DATE DUE

| | | | |
|---|---|---|---|
| | | | |
| | | | |
| | | | |
| | | | |
| | | | |
| | | | |
| | | | |
| | | | |
| | | | |
| | | | |
| | | | |
| | | | |

DEMCO

Critical Thinking About
Environmental Issues

# Pesticides

Other books in the Critical Thinking About Environmental Issues series are:

Endangered Species
Global Warming

Critical Thinking About
Environmental Issues

# Pesticides

By Samantha Beres

**GREENHAVEN
PRESS ®**

**THOMSON**
™
**GALE**

San Diego • Detroit • New York • San Francisco • Cleveland
New Haven, Conn. • Waterville, Maine • London • Munich

LIBRARY OF CONGRESS CATALOGING-IN-PUBLICATION DATA

Beres, Samantha.
    Pesticides / Samantha Beres
       p. cm. — (Critical thinking about environmental issues series)
Summary: Examines the controversy over the use of pesticides and discusses the effects of this use on agriculture, health, and the environment.
Includes bibliographical references (p.   ).
    ISBN 0-7377-1272-4 (hardback : alk. paper)
1. Pesticides—United States—Juvenile literature. 2. Pesticides—Environmental aspects—United States—Juvenile literature. 3. Pesticides—Health aspects—United States—Juvenile literature. [1. Pesticides.] I. Title. II. Series.
    SB950.2.A1 B47 2002
    363.17'92—dc21

                                   2002000383

# Contents

# Foreword

If a nation expects to be ignorant and free ... it expects what never was and never will be.

Thomas Jefferson

Thomas Jefferson understood that a free nation depends on an educated citizenry. Citizens must have the level of knowledge necessary to make informed decisions on complex public policy issues. In the United States, schools have a major responsibility for developing that knowledge.

In the twenty-first century, American citizens will struggle with environmental questions of the first order. These include complicated and contentious topics such as global warming, pesticide use, and species extinction. The goal of this series, Critical Thinking About Environmental Issues, is to help young people recognize the complexity of these topics and help them view the issues analytically and objectively.

All too often, environmental problems are treated as moral issues. For example, using pesticides is often considered bad because residues may be found on food and because the application of pesticides may harm birds. In contrast, relying on organic food (produced without insecticides or herbicides) is considered good. Yet this simplistic approach fails to recognize the role of pesticides in producing food for the world and ignores the scientific studies that suggest that pesticides cause little harm to humans. Such superficial treatment of multifaceted issues does not serve citizens well and provides a poor basis for education.

This series, Critical Thinking About Environmental Issues, exposes students to the complexities of each issue it addresses. While the books touch on many aspects of each environmental problem, their goal is primarily to point out the differences in scientific opinion surrounding the topics. These books present the facts that underlie different scientific interpretations. They also address differing values that may affect the interpretation of the facts and economic questions that may affect policy choices.

The goal of the series is to open up inquiry on issues that are often viewed too narrowly. Each book, written in language that is understandable to young readers, provides enough information about the scientific theories and methods for the reader to weigh the merits of the leading arguments. Ultimately, students, like adult citizens, will make their own decisions.

With environmental issues, especially those where new science is always emerging, the possibility exists that there is not enough information to settle the issue. If this is the case, the books may spur readers to pursue the topics further. If readers come away from this series critically examining their own opinions as well as others' and eager to seek more information, the goal of these books will have been achieved.

by Jane S. Shaw
Series Editor

# INTRODUCTION

For years, farmers have tried to halt the devastation to their crops caused by insects, weeds, and other pests. Until the twentieth century, they relied on crude mixtures based on poisons such as lead and arsenic. These didn't work on very many crops, and they were dangerous to humans. But they improved the ability of farmers to provide food for a growing population.

The modern era of pesticides began when sophisticated synthetic pesticides—made by scientists combining chemicals in a laboratory —were developed. DDT (dichlorodiphenyltrichloroethane) was first applied during the Second World War. Unlike most previous pesticides, it appeared to pose no harm to humans. It was heralded as a miracle chemical, and started a drive for similar pesticides.

But over the years the use of the new pesticides caused problems, especially because they were applied so extensively. People began to notice that birds died after the chemicals were sprayed. They discovered that DDT remained in the environment for years without breaking down into harmless components. A landmark book, *Silent Spring* by Rachel Carson, alerted the world to the potential dangers of pesticides, especially DDT.

Campaigns against pesticides continue today. These campaigns involve both facts and emotions. Pesticides are poisons that can harm birds and other wildlife if they are not monitored carefully. Some are dangerous to humans. Yet the world's farmers are using insecticides, herbicides, and related pest killers on crops that are feeding the world's growing population, now more than 6 billion. Public health officials are using pesticides to attack malaria, which kills at least 1 million people a year, many of them children.

Pesticides are regulated by government officials, who face controversy over whether to allow pesticides to be used, and for what purposes. All decision makers who make policies about pesticides need the facts. They need scientific knowledge about the effects—positive and negative—of pesticides and economic knowledge about the consequences of using or not using them. Frequently these facts are ignored or overwhelmed by emotion and political conflict.

The purpose of this book is to look beyond the emotional rhetoric and dispassionately examine the factual basis for arguments about pesticides. The facts to be examined are scientific but also political and economic.

*Because exposure to pesticides can be harmful, many workers wear protective gear while handling them.*

The issues surrounding pesticides suggest that there is no simple yes or no answer about their use. Perhaps there will continue to be a place for pesticides in the future, but one more limited than that of today. New techniques of food production may make it easier to reduce or eliminate the use of pesticides, and pesticides may become safer in the future than they are today. This book will explore the possibilities.

Students, who are future voters, consumers, and decision makers, have an opportunity to look objectively at this issue. Without a vested interest in either side of the argument, they can develop an understanding of the facts that underlie the controversies.

# CHAPTER 1

# Why the Controversy over Pesticide Use?

I t is an everyday occurrence. A woman in the midwestern United States sprays her rosebushes to kill aphids. Cotton farmers in California fight the insidious boll weevil. In Mozambique, children sleep under nets that have been treated to protect them against disease-carrying mosquitoes.

All are using pesticides, chemicals designed to kill destructive pests such as insects, weeds, and fungi. These chemicals have helped save crops all over the world from destruction, yet they may be harming the environment and endangering human health. As a result, some people wonder if these chemicals should be used on crops and in people's homes.

## Pesticides Today

The term *pesticide* covers three major types of chemicals. Herbicides, which kill weeds, are the most widely used. Next come insecticides, which kill insects, and then fungicides, which kill molds that grow on fruits and vegetables. Not all farmers use pesticides. The vast majority of insecticides are applied to just two crops, cotton and corn, and the majority of herbicides are used to kill weeds that compete with corn and soybeans. Even so, the quantities are substantial. Over 90 percent of the major fruit crops such as grapes, oranges, and apples, are treated with at least one pesticide.

*A worker sprays pesticides on grapevines. Pesticides are commonly used in agriculture.*

Although the modern era of pesticides began in the twentieth century, pesticides in some form have been around for more than two thousand years. As early as 200 B.C., the ancient Greeks used sulfur (sometimes combined with oil and pitch) to kill insects on crops. Throughout the centuries, poisonous elements such as mercury and arsenic have been used as pesticides. In the seventeenth century, some insecticides were made from plants, including an extract from tobacco leaves and, later, an extract from chrysanthemum flowers. In the nineteenth century, metal compounds became popular among American and European farmers.

Pesticides kill by interfering with the vital processes of weeds, insects, and organisms that cause plant diseases, such as fungi and nematodes. Different pesticides work in different ways. Some affect the nervous system of insects, and others block the photosynthesis by which weeds grow. Today most pesticides are synthetic (man-made) compounds, made by combining chemicals. Once chemists find that some substances are harmful to pests, they can modify these substances to enhance certain effects and eliminate others.

## DDT, a New Kind of Pesticide

At the end of World War II, the advent of DDT revolutionized pesticide use, opening up enormous possibilities for killing pests on cotton and other crops. It also provided a way to kill mosquitoes that carried disease, especially malaria. "DDT did seem to be an ideal material," writes Thomas Dunlap in his book on DDT. "To many it marked the beginning of a new era."[1]

DDT (whose full chemical name is dichlorodiphenyltrichloroethane) is a compound made of carbon and hydrogen that was first synthesized in 1874. Its potency as an insect killer was discovered in 1939 by Swiss scientist Paul Muller. World War II began in Europe that same year, and the U.S. government began searching for a way to stop the spread of insect-borne diseases among troops. The U.S.

*Scientist Paul Muller discovered the effectiveness of DDT as an insecticide in 1939.*

Department of Agriculture (USDA) developed a powder containing 10 percent DDT.

The agency's find was well timed. Typhus, a disease carried by body lice, broke out in Italy and could have easily spread among soldiers, who lived in crowded, dirty conditions. All over Europe, stations were set up where soldiers could dust their bodies, clothes, and bedding, killing body lice for weeks. The typhus episode ended within a year.

DDT was different from previous poisons used to combat lice and insects. The earlier pesticides were "rather brute instruments, short-lived in their efficacy, and requiring repeated applications by hand," says Christopher J. Bosso, who has studied the history of DDT. "They were acutely toxic to their users."[2] In contrast, DDT caused no acute reaction to the individual, and its impact on pests lasted a long time, so it didn't have to be sprayed continually. DDT was found to be effective against lice (typhus carriers), fleas (plague carriers), and mosquitoes (malaria, dengue fever, and yellow fever carriers).

After the war, the success of DDT opened up a new world for homeowners, farmers, and foresters, many of whom became avid DDT users in the United States. Partly through financial support from the USDA, farmers began killing pests such as boll weevils that were destroying cotton crops, and the government itself began spraying pesticides on forests to kill destructive gypsy moths. Much of the spraying was carried out by low-flying planes that doused farms, forests, and suburbs. In 1944, sales of DDT amounted to $10 million, mostly for military use. By 1951, sales exceeded $110 million, mostly because of agriculture.

The sudden embrace of DDT bothered some scientists, who recognized that the chemical being sprayed throughout the country had not been tested thoroughly. It was known that large doses could cause symptoms such as tremors and aching joints and that it accumulated in the body. Says Thomas Dunlap, "Although the new chemical seemed a wonderful substitute for lead arsenate, it was not without its dangers."[3] Yet it caused no visible harm to people at low doses and it required only small quantities to be effective. These facts overwhelmed caution.

Other parts of the world began using DDT to combat malaria, a deadly disease. Huts and homes in North Africa and Asia were sprayed, and initial success was great. The number of malaria cases went down drastically.

*Prior to DDT spraying, the boll weevil devastated cotton crops.*

In Sri Lanka, an island country south of India formerly called Ceylon, there were 2.8 million cases of malaria in 1946. By 1963, DDT had brought the number of cases down to 17. When the country stopped using DDT, the number of cases shot back up to 2.5 million. In Zanzibar, an island off the east coast of Africa, the portion of the populace with malaria dropped from 70 percent in 1958 to 5 percent in 1964. However, because use of DDT declined, the incidence of malaria was back up to between 50 and 60 percent by 1984. According to estimates by the World Health Organization, during the period of DDT's use approximately 25 million lives were saved.

## A Change of Heart

In retrospect, the USDA may have brought about the demise of DDT. The department took up aerial spraying almost with abandon and it did not carefully monitor or research the possible harms that the pesticide could cause. Congress provided funds for spraying but not for background research that would help understand how it might affect species other than the ones it was aimed at. When the USDA sprayed over swamps and forests where there were few people, little outcry occurred. But when it moved to urban areas, people could see the results—dead birds among them.

Furthermore, when farmers who wanted to grow their crops without pesticides complained that the spraying was contaminating their fields, the government ignored them. Some organic gardeners even went to court, but the courts agreed with the federal government that the spraying had an important public purpose that overrode what appeared then to be a small harm.

Eventually, the spraying campaigns caused a reaction. When people noticed dead birds scattered on yards or observed that fewer birds lived in their areas, they could not help but wonder, could the spraying of pesticides be at fault?

Olga and Stuart Huckins, owners of a two-acre private bird sanctuary in Duxbury, Massachusetts, were certain of it. In the summer of 1957, directly after the area was sprayed for mosquitoes, they noticed dead songbirds scattered across the sanctuary. Olga wrote a detailed letter to the *Boston Herald* and sent a copy and a note to her friend Rachel Carson, who had worked for the U.S. Fish and Wildlife Service for sixteen years. Huckins hoped that her friend could do something about the spraying. Carson, disturbed by the news, spent the next four and one-half years researching evidence that pesticides were harming wildlife and the environment. The research led to her book, *Silent Spring.*

Rachel Carson was a biologist by training but her real strength had always been her writing. After composing several best-sellers, including *The Sea Around Us,* she published *Silent Spring* as a series of articles in the *New Yorker* magazine. When the book itself was published in 1962, the public's view of DDT and pesticides was forever changed.

## *Silent Spring*

*Silent Spring* starts with a dramatic fictitious account of a world in which everything is dying, where "only silence lay over the fields and woods and marsh."[4] Carson then presents actual incidents of harm that appear to have been caused by pesticides. These were primarily accounts of dead birds and other wildlife apparently killed by aerial sprays.

*Rachel Carson
revealed effects of
pesticides on wildlife
and the environment.*

Carson reported on one pesticide-related event after another, incidents involving many different insecticides, not just DDT. She said the link between the impact and the effect was suspicious but not conclusive, and cited many cases of broadside spraying. For example, in southeastern Michigan in the fall of 1959, the USDA dusted twenty-seven thousand acres with pellets of aldrin, a pesticide somewhat related to DDT, to control the Japanese beetle. In 1954, another pesticide, dieldrin, was sprayed from the air across fourteen hundred acres in eastern Illinois. In the 1950s, DDT was used to kill elm bark beetles, which carried the fungus that causes Dutch elm disease.

Carson was probably accurate in claiming that the USDA knew little about these chemicals. She said about the department's fire ant program: "In short, the Department of Agriculture embarked on its program without even elementary investigation of what was already known about the chemical to be used—or if it investigated, it ignored the findings." [5] Indiscriminate spraying and excessive use may have had more to do with the charges of environmental harm than the pesticides themselves. Almost lost in the debates that followed the publication of *Silent Spring* was the fact that pesticide use had increased suddenly and dramatically, thanks especially to the USDA.

## Response to *Silent Spring*

*Silent Spring* is largely a potpourri of incidents and stories from which it is difficult to extricate the facts (scientists have been trying ever since it was published). Although the book was eagerly read by the public, it was also harshly criticized. Much of the criticism was the emotional reaction of people heavily involved in the manufacture of and reliance on a "miracle chemical" that had suddenly become an evil nemesis. Thus, they called Carson an alarmist and said her approach was manipulative, tugging on the readers' emotions rather than presenting a fair and balanced case.

Most critics did not challenge the examples that Carson cited but argued that the benefits of greater crop production that pesticides provided outweighed the possible harms. In 1971 at a hearing on tighter pesticide regulation, William Hazeltine, an entomologist with the Mosquito Abatement District in Oroville, California, testified. Still stinging from the impact of *Silent Spring*, he argued that the public had been misled. "I contrast the predictions of doom and disaster with what I see: healthy people, living longer lives with more leisure. Yet the doom is repeatedly told from every corner."[6]

## A Political Revolution

Efforts to ban DDT started in the 1960s, largely as a result of Carson's book. Responding to the emerging concern about pesticides and other pollutants that affected the air and water, President Nixon created the Environmental Protection Agency (EPA) in 1970. "In fact, EPA today may be said without exaggeration to be the extended shadow of Rachel Carson," wrote one commentator years later in a journal published by the EPA. "The influence of her book has brought together over 14,000 scientists, lawyers, managers, and other employees across the country to fight the good fight for environmental protection."[7]

It did not take long for the new agency to go after DDT. The agency conducted hearings in Washington, D.C., in 1971 and 1972. The hearings lasted for seven months, during which time 125 witnesses were called. Yet the scientific evidence against DDT was not extremely strong, and the administrative judge, Edmund Sweeney, denied the ban. He said that "DDT is not a carcinogenic hazard to man," and the "evidence in this proceeding supports the conclusion that there is a present need for the essential uses of DDT."[8] In spite of this recommendation, the newly appointed EPA administrator William Ruckelshaus decided to support the ban. DDT has not been used in the United States, except in emergencies, ever since.

## The *Silent Spring* Legacy

*Silent Spring* revolutionized public attitudes and political treatment of pesticides. Banning DDT helped launch the modern environmental movement. Of course, other problems such as air and water pollution also galvanized the movement in the late 1960s, culminating in nationwide demonstrations on the first Earth Day in April 1970. But fear of chemicals was an important motivator.

It is now forty years since *Silent Spring* was published. Science has supplied far more information about pesticides than Carson had when she wrote her book, and pesticides have improved in many ways since 1962, perhaps in part because of the alarm she raised. Excessive use of these chemicals appears to have ended long ago.

On one topic, whether DDT contributed to a decline of birds of prey such as eagles, falcons, and hawks, most scientists agree that Carson was correct. Subsequent studies have confirmed her findings.

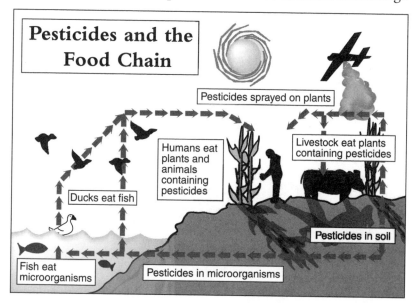

**Pesticides and the Food Chain**

Pesticides sprayed on plants

Livestock eat plants containing pesticides

Humans eat plants and animals containing pesticides

Ducks eat fish

Pesticides in soil

Fish eat microorganisms

Pesticides in microorganisms

It appears that raptors suffer from the effects of DDT. These are birds of prey, which kill and eat smaller birds, many of which survive by eating fish. Because raptors are at the top of the food chain, they accumulate small amounts of DDT in their systems. Gradually, these amounts add up, apparently causing the birds' eggshells to become thin. Eventually, the eggshells are so thin that few offspring can survive, because the shells break prematurely.

Raptors are physiologically more sensitive to DDT than other types of birds. One study found that songbirds or game birds with the same level of DDT contamination had eggshell thickness that had decreased by only 1 percent compared with 15 percent for the raptors.

The case against DDT is not exactly open-and-shut, even now, but the circumstantial evidence against it is very strong. It remains possible that contaminants other than DDT—some that were less noticed and less studied, such as polychlorinated biphenyls (PCBs)—were working to reduce bird populations. And there is some evidence that raptors weren't disappearing as fast as most people thought.

A comparison of the annual Christmas Bird Counts conducted by the National Audubon Society between 1941 (before DDT was used in the United States) and 1960 (as DDT's use was waning) reveals that at least twenty-six different species of birds became more, not less, numerous during the decades of greatest DDT usage. For example, only 197 bald eagles were documented in 1941; the number had increased to 891 in 1960. However, birding developed over that period and more birdwatchers were probably scouting for them in 1960.

The impact of DDT on raptors may have been primarily an American phenomenon. One British writer points out that the United Kingdom never experienced that kind of widespread environmental impact from DDT. He explains that the government authorities "considered they could not afford the massive blanket spraying programs which were characteristic of the use of DDT and related compounds in the United States of America."[9]

Even so, the evidence has persuaded many scientists that DDT is the major culprit behind eggshell thinning. In 2000, the National Research Council, a prestigious group of scholars, reported that pes-

*Cartons of thinned peregrine falcon eggshells appear to be the result of the birds' exposure to DDT.*

ticides like DDT "led to the thinning and breaking of the eggshells" of peregrine falcons, ospreys, and brown pelicans. "Since the banning of DDT, most of the predatory-bird populations have recovered substantially." [10] Most people believe that the gradual disappearance of DDT in the water led to the comeback of these birds.

## Assessing DDT

DDT was a highly unusual chemical. The harm it caused stemmed from the fact that it does not easily break down into its components. It is very persistent, lasting in the environment for years and accumulating in the bodies of birds at the top of the food chain.

Some pesticides chemically related to DDT, such as aldrin and dieldrin, are also persistent, but others are not. Malathion and carbaryl, for example, are widely used insecticides that do not accumulate in the bodies of fish or other animals. And like DDT, they appear to have low toxicity for humans.

On issues other than the harm to birds, Carson's claims have not survived scientific scrutiny so well. Perhaps the most alarming part of *Silent Spring* was the implication that pesticides, including DDT, cause cancer. Carson did not come right out and make that claim; she was actually somewhat vague. Rather, she asked whether we can possibly define a safe dose of pesticides when there are so many cancer-causing agents in our environment that can work together to cause disease.

Today, the evidence that DDT causes cancer in humans is weak. Even though it accumulates in human fat, its effects have not been proven to cause cancer. For example, a 1989 study published in the *American Journal of Public Health* followed nearly one thousand people for twenty-five years to determine if those with higher levels of DDT had higher cancer mortality. The subjects of the study, residents of Charleston, South Carolina, were chosen because they had shown traces of DDT in their blood. As people in the study died, the cause of death was determined, as was the level of DDT in their systems. The levels in the subjects who died of cancer were on average lower than the levels found in those who died of other causes. Thus the authors found "no relation between either overall mortal-

*Although pesticides may prevent infestations such as grasshopper swarms, the public continues to debate their use.*

ity or cancer mortality and increasing serum DDT levels [levels of DDT in body fluids]."[11]

# A Continuing Controversy

Although it would be wrong to give Rachel Carson sole responsibility for the ban on DDT or today's fear of chemicals, *Silent Spring* launched a backlash against chemicals and even against technology that continues. This backlash has had both positive and negative results.

On the positive side, the alarm Carson raised gradually changed the regulation of pesticides, which previously was in the hands of the USDA, a government agency that saw its role as promoting the growth of crops (and also the growth of trees). The agency enthusiastically promoted pesticide use, although few, if any, scientists studied and monitored the environmental effects. Regulation changed when the EPA was given responsibility for supervising pesticides. The agency's director, William Ruckelshaus, chose to make the ban on DDT his first important act. "The issue was a test of the EPA's willingness to take strong action,"[12] says Thomas Dunlap.

In addition, the environmental movement, launched in part by the fight over DDT, mobilized public action. This had a cascade of results, from the passage of new laws to voluntary programs to pick up litter and clean up streams. Hostility to dangerous chemicals, and lobbying to prohibit their use, has been a hallmark of environmental activism, partly because of DDT's history.

An unfortunate result of the alarm was to give DDT, in particular, and pesticides in general a "satanic image."[13] Many people reflexively oppose the use of pesticides as if there are no benefits in wiping out grasshoppers, mosquitoes, weeds, and disease. Today, remarks author Elizabeth Whelan, "the majority of Americans are vaguely convinced that DDT was the ultimate in dangerous pesticides and unaware of the millions of lives the chemical saved."[14]

So, when a report surfaces that a pesticide such as methyl bromide hurts the environment, the battle lines are drawn. On one side are those who assume that it should be banned; on the other, those who want to keep it whatever the cost. Today, many people still share an all-or-nothing attitude about pesticides.

# CHAPTER 2

# Pesticides and Human Health

E ver since *Silent Spring*, there have been two major concerns about the environmental impact of pesticides. One is that they may kill birds and other wildlife. The other is that they may be causing cancer and other diseases in humans.

Judging by research, newspaper reports, and legislation, the question of human health rather than the impact on animals is uppermost in people's minds, at least in the United States. "Public concern regarding the role of environmental pollutants in causing human cancer remains intense," says Clark W. Heath Jr., writing in the journal *Cancer*, "and for no specific class of potential pollutant is concern more intense than for chemical pesticides."[15]

## Pesticide Poisoning

The most obvious danger to human health from pesticides is through accidental poisonings. But what seems to worry people more is that long-term exposures to extremely small quantities of pesticides may be harmful. Some experts argue that tiny amounts of pesticides in the foods people eat could lead to cancer and other illnesses that develop over a long period of exposure.

Certainly, most poisoning occurs in a single accidental dose, not through slow accumulation of tiny quantities. According to the American Association of Poison Control Centers, seventy-nine thousand children in the United States were involved in household pesticide-related poisonings in 1999, the latest year for which statistics are available. A study of thirty-seven children who had been hospitalized at Children's Medical Center in Dallas as a result of pesticide poisoning found that 73 percent of the children had swallowed the chemicals. Most of the poisonings occurred because of careless storage of pesticides in the home.

Direct exposure can also occur when pesticides are transported by air. People who live in agricultural communities can breathe in poison dust from sprayed crops. For example, in 1999 a mist from a weed-killing pesticide blew from a 160-acre field into the small California town of Earlimart, and 150 people were forced to evacuate their homes and offices. Twenty-nine were sent to the hospital suffering from vomiting, headaches, nausea, burning eyes, and shortness of breath—typical symptoms of pesticide poisoning.

Even less frequently, accidents stem from eating food with pesticides. In 1985, one thousand people in the United States and Canada became ill within twelve hours of eating watermelons. The melons had residues of Temik.

## Chronic Exposures

For the most part, these are isolated incidents and involve consuming extraordinarily high doses of pesticides. Although these incidents fuel

*Wearing protective suits, technicians collect soil samples to determine if toxins are present.*

alarm about the presence of poisons, the major concern today revolves around fear that typical consumers, and especially children, may be threatened by pesticide residues in foods—in parts per million or parts per billion. These are the trace amounts that may be left on the surface of fruits and vegetables. "Although some health workers may be familiar with the management of acute pesticide poisoning, chronic effects of pesticide exposures are often overlooked," writes Gina Solomon in a booklet for health care personnel, "Pesticides and Health." [16]

The chief fear is that these residues may cause cancer if enough are ingested over a long period. Fear can even turn to panic. In 1989, an environmental organization charged publicly that Alar, a chemical used on apples, caused cancer. Even though this was not confirmed—and even though Alar was used on only a small portion of all apples—the claim caused an uproar. Headlines blared the news. The television show *60 Minutes* featured the charge, and popular actress Meryl Streep appeared on television expressing her alarm.

In response, terrified parents threw out their children's apple juice and the New York City school district stopped selling apples. The fears were overblown. Three government agencies, including the EPA, issued statements within days saying that apples were safe. But the producer pulled the product from the market and it hasn't been used since.

No scare of such magnitude has occurred with pesticides since then. (Alar was not really a pesticide; it was a chemical that kept apples from falling off trees before they were ripe, but because it was a chemical used in agriculture, it came under EPA regulation.) But the fear lingers.

People forget that chemicals can be either natural or synthetic (man-made). Bruce Ames is a biochemist who used to be worried about cancer-causing substances in the environment. He became famous for inventing a laboratory test that screens substances to see if they might be carcinogenic. It's called the Ames test. But over the years he has become much more relaxed about this problem.

Having studied both synthetic and natural chemicals, Ames points out that plants make their own poisons to ward off pests. These are "natural" pesticides. He and his associate Lois Swirsky Gold estimate that people ingest (that is, eat or breathe in) about ten thousand times more natural pesticides than they do synthetic ones.

"Almost all the world is natural chemicals," says Ames. "A cup of coffee is filled with chemicals." In fact, he explains, a cup of coffee

*Government agencies conduct frequent studies to analyze the quantity and toxicity of pesticide residues in the environment.*

has one thousand chemicals, only twenty-two of which have been analyzed in a laboratory. Of those twenty-two, seventeen were found to be carcinogens. "There are 10 milligrams of known carcinogens in a cup of coffee and that's more carcinogens than you're likely to get from pesticide residues for a year!"[17] says Ames. That doesn't mean people should stop drinking coffee. His point is that there are many cancer-causing substances in our diets, but many are natural.

Even synthetic pesticides are not found on food in large quantities. The U.S. Food and Drug Administration (FDA), a government agency, conducts a study called the Total Diet Study four times a year. FDA officials monitor foods to determine if they have residues of pesticides, minerals, and other possibly toxic substances. The agency examines more than two hundred food items representative of Americans' diets. The residues found in the foods are compared with the allowable doses of the chemicals on foods that have been established by the EPA.

In 1999, 9,438 samples were analyzed, including both domestic and imported foods. No residues that violated the EPA standards were found in 99.2 percent of all domestic samples and no excessive residues were found in 96.9 percent of the imports.

But this monitoring system has come under fire. The federal government "analyzes a single pesticide at a time," says Erik Olson, an attorney with the Natural Resources Defense Council. "If you pick up a piece of celery or an apple or some other commodity, you may be eating residues of multiple pesticides—five, seven, eight, nine different pesticide residues may be on that apple."[18] Sandra Bell of Friends of the Earth says that government testing "neglects the fact that in reality you're exposed to a number of pesticides in an average meal that you eat. It's the way those pesticides interact with each other that could be of concern."[19]

Another criticism comes from a 1992 government report that said that the FDA does not sample enough foods—less than 1 percent of domestic and imported food is tested—and that it tests for only about one-third of the pesticides in existence. Yet another complaint is that the FDA is too slow. By the time test results are finished, the food has been sold and eaten.

Although these comments show that the FDA findings should be viewed with caution, they don't cancel out the fact that the FDA has found low residues of pesticides on food. The question remains, could these residues be harmful?

## Do Pesticides Cause Cancer?

The chief question that troubles people is whether these low levels of pesticides scattered throughout our environment may be causing cancer. To determine whether this concern is justified, there are really two questions to be answered.

The first is whether pesticides contribute significantly to the levels of cancer in the population taken as a whole. How do they compare with say, smoking tobacco or inherited characteristics? The other question is whether specific pesticides, if taken in small doses over a long time, can cause cancer. (Even if the overall impact of pesticides is slight, it could still be dangerous to ingest small quantities of a chemical over many years.)

One of the most comprehensive attempts to address the first question was conducted by the National Cancer Institute of Canada, an organization formed by the Department of National Health and Welfare and the Canadian Cancer Society. The institute hosted a panel of cancer experts to examine the possible contribution of pesticide exposure to cancer in humans. They evaluated more than sev-

*Researchers are still trying to determine if people who regularly handle pesticides are more likely to develop cancer.*

enty published studies about exposure to pesticides on foods as well as exposure through home and garden use.

The panel's 1997 report said it was "not aware of any definitive evidence to suggest that synthetic pesticides contribute significantly to overall cancer mortality."[20] The Canadian panel substantiated its finding by reporting that cancer risk overall had not increased over the past ten years.

Others have found the same. In a famous study in 1986, two prominent researchers, Richard Doll and Richard Peto, concluded that all environmental factors (that is, contaminants in the air, water, food, and land) contributed no more than 2 percent of all cancer deaths. Pesticides represent a small portion of that 2 percent.

The Canadian panel did recommend that research continue. It also expressed concern that farmworkers may be more at risk for cancer because of their frequent contact with herbicides. And it suggested that DDT, which persists in the environment, might be linked to chronic disease. The overall thrust of these findings was that pesticides are not likely to have much impact on overall incidence of cancer.

Their findings, while reassuring, do not answer the second question, whether pesticides can cause cancer in individuals exposed to small quantities over a long time. Determining whether a specific pesticide or other chemical causes cancer is difficult.

To begin with, the causes of cancer are poorly understood. "Most laypeople probably don't understand that in *all* cases it is impossible to say for sure how someone got cancer," says Michael Fumento, author of a book on the misuse of science. If a person gets lung cancer after smoking all his or her life, "it's a good bet" that the cigarettes caused it, but "that is by no means certain,"[21] he says.

Second, if a substance does cause cancer, it usually takes an extremely long time to develop, and many other things could have contributed to the cancer. It is difficult to make a link, partly because "too many other factors get in the way."[22] Many forces contribute to disease, ranging from inherited characteristics to viruses and bacteria, and pinpointing a specific environmental pollutant can be like finding a needle in a haystack.

Scientists try to determine whether a substance causes cancer or other harms such as birth defects by studying populations that have been exposed to the substance and seeing if they have higher than normal levels of cancer or defects. A branch of medicine known as epidemiology attempts to find such cause-and-effect relationships. "Epidemiology is a science of association," writes Fumento, introducing the basic tenets of epidemiology. It combines statistical information with knowledge about how an illness or accident occurs. "The purpose is to detect what is causing the problem and how great the problem is."[23] But the statistics that form the basis of the study must be scrutinized with a keen eye.

Fumento tells a couple of stories to explain the difficulties that arise with epidemiological studies. Suppose a woman has a miscarriage; that is, her unborn baby dies a few months after conception. Her doctor does not know what caused the miscarriage, but she demands a reason. She had taken a prescribed medicine for morning sickness, and she finds out that other women who have taken this prescription also miscarried. She calls a reporter, who finds more cases of miscarriages that may be linked to the prescription drug. Suddenly, newspapers nationwide warn pregnant women not to take it.

What the woman, the reporter, and possibly the doctor do not know is that miscarriages are common (up to one-third of all pregnant women will miscarry). Furthermore, the causes of miscarriages are generally unknown.

Fumento offers another illustration of the pitfalls in trying to determine cause and effect. Let's say that city records show that eighty-nine people have died since a new factory came to town. A newspaper reporter wonders if the chemicals produced by the factory have led to these deaths, but then the reporter discovers that about ninety people die each year in that town.

The difficulties lead epidemiologists to try to find groups of people that have been heavily exposed to a chemical, such as workers in factories that have high levels of the substance being studied. If cancer turns up in these workers at levels higher than expected for the population as a whole, the chemical may be the cause. Several chemicals used as pesticides have been found to be carcinogenic this way. They include arsenic, benzene, and chromium.

To find cancer-causing substances, scientists take another approach as well. They study the effects of chemicals fed to laboratory animals such as rats and mice. If the rats or mice develop tumors (abnormal growths or lesions), there is a possibility that under comparable conditions humans might also. And if the growths are malignant (that is, if they are cancerous), then there is reason to believe that the substances under study may be carcinogenic in humans, too.

*Scientists examine the effects of chemicals injected into mice to find out if they will cause cancer in humans.*

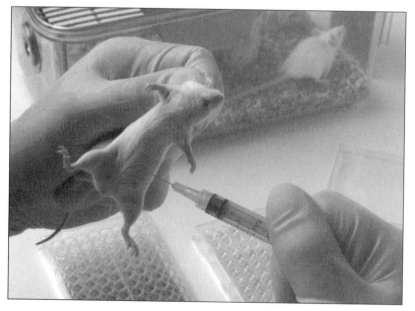

Scientists work with only a small number of rats or mice at one time, yet their goal is to find out if a chemical will cause cancer when millions of people are exposed to it. If cancer doesn't show up in a test of one hundred mice, it still may turn up in the human population if millions use the chemical. So the researchers feed the animals much more of the chemical than people would ever be exposed to. The laboratory animals are given what is called the maximum tolerated dose, or MTD. This is the amount of pesticide (or other substance being tested) that the rat can be fed safely—that is, without dying from acute poisoning. If the substance is cancer-causing, then over time this amount will cause tumors in some of the animals.

But such tests are controversial. For one thing, the dose itself may be fatal or severely harmful to the rats or mice. Bruce N. Ames and his associate Lois Swirsky Gold point out that "testing at near-toxic levels frequently can cause chronic cell killing and consequent cell replacement."[24] That itself can lead to cancer, they say.

Second, it's not always clear what these findings tell us about people. The chemical Alar, which caused such a panic in 1989, was put on the "cancer suspect list" because a laboratory test showed that animals that had ingested Alar developed tumors. The animals had been fed a diet that was between 0.5 and 1 percent Alar. Although this sounds like a small portion, it would be difficult for a human to consume a diet that was 1 percent Alar. Given the tiny amounts of Alar that remained on apples (and not on all apples, either) a person would need to eat twenty-eight thousand pounds of apples daily for ten years to parallel what the lab animals were fed. Because one apple does not even equal a pound, that would be a lot of apples. "The rat tests mislead the public. They may communicate some useful information to the experts, but they have misled the public on the real cancer risks in our lives,"[25] says one animal-test skeptic, Dennis Avery.

## Different Pesticides, Different Concerns

In 1993, *Pesticides in the Diets of Infants and Children,* a report by the National Academy of Sciences' National Research Council, recommended that U.S. pesticide laws be overhauled to make foods safer for children. "The current system for regulating pesticide residues for foods in the United States needs to be fundamentally restructured so that the health concerns become a priority, especially when it comes to children,"[26] wrote Philip J. Landrigan, the pediatrician who headed the committee. That report led to changes in pesticide regulation.

The report based its conclusions on several facts: Children eat more produce (fruits and vegetables) per pound of body weight than adults, they have less variety in their diets, and they may eat more of certain processed foods. The report triggered unanimous passage in 1996 of the Food Quality Protection Act, which requires the EPA to review all pesticides and tighten the amount of exposure allowed to make them safer for young children.

Although the National Research Council report changed government policy, some question its validity. For example, the study identifies upward trends of cancers and birth defects in children, but Kenneth Chilton and Stephen Huebner point out that environmental contaminants "have not been established as one of the top risks to children's health."[27] No one has so far explained these trends in children's diseases.

Nor, they say, did the authors of the report weigh the risks of pesticide use against the benefits of a diverse and abundant food supply—a food supply that pesticides help to make available. They also argue that children are exposed to far greater dangers, and that concentrating too much on a remotely possible harm from pesticide residues shifts attention from the real killers—accidents. Accidents account for 40 percent of the deaths of children between the ages of one and fourteen.

Although the National Research Council report was mostly about pesticide residues in foods, it did offer studies and incidents suggesting that some children may be at a higher risk of illness from other pesticide exposures than are older people. For example, after a carpeted apartment was treated for fleas, the vapors in an infant's breathing zone (up to approximately ten inches above the carpet throughout the house) were substantially higher than an adult's breathing zone, even though the windows were open. The study also reported that wooden playground equipment may expose children to pesticides because 20 percent of wooden structures in California parks are treated with chemicals.

Concerns about pesticide residues must be kept in perspective. If either adults or children avoid eating fruits and vegetables because of the remote possibility of pesticide residues, their health may be harmed. Fruits and vegetables have fiber, carbohydrates, and the vitamins necessary to maintain health.

Ironically, there is even evidence that eating some fruits and vegetables may reduce cancer. In a National Research Council study, carotene [plural-carotenes] found in carrots and many orange and dark-green leafy vegetables appeared to reduce the incidence of skin, breast, bladder, and various other cancers. Stomach cancer has dropped by 75 percent over the past forty years, and some contend that this may be due to an increase in vitamin C. "At present, a sound recommendation for cancer prevention is to increase fruit and vegetable intake,"[28] says another report of the National Research Council titled *Carcinogens and Anticarcinogens in the Human Diet.* Pesticides help keep fruits and vegetables on supermarket shelves.

## New Concerns

Periodically, new worries arise about the health effects of pesticides. For example, a book called *Our Stolen Future* contends that some pesticides, including DDT, which still lingers in the environment, may be acting like estrogen, a female hormone, on the human body. The authors speculate that such chemicals in the environment may harm the reproductive systems of males. A number of studies have attempted to link exposure of pesticides to a low sperm count in men. One study interviewed 225 men from a farming region in Argentina who had been exposed to pesticides in their work. Luc Multigner of the French research team concluded that "exposure to pesticides and solvents" was "significantly associated"[29] with low sperm values.

Yet, as with all epidemiological studies, care must be taken. Low sperm counts can be caused by other things such as a lack of iodine, thyroid problems, or depression. And it's hard to know whether sperm counts are declining generally. To determine whether sperm counts are going down, scientists must have reliable information about what sperm counts were in the past. But information about pre-1970 sperm counts is shaky, says statistician Bjørn Lomborg.

Recent studies have suggested that the combination of two widely used agricultural chemicals, the herbicide paraquat and the fungicide maneb, which are applied to millions of acres of farmland each year, causes Parkinson's disease. Also under scrutiny is atrazine, currently the most extensively applied agricultural herbicide in the United States. Studies have shown atrazine to cause cancer in laboratory animals. And benlate, a fungicide, has been linked to severe birth defects.

Each allegation should be studied, but to jump from claim to conclusion would be premature. The National Research Council conducted a four-year assessment of the toxicity of hormone-like chemicals, some of which may be found in pesticides. Panel member James C. Lamb IV, a consulting toxicologist, says, "We couldn't find any clear evidence that people had been harmed by typical environmental exposures to hormonally active chemicals."[30]

## Pesticides and Farmworkers

There is one pesticide threat that does seem clear—the threat to agricultural workers who spray pesticides on crops. According to the American Association of Poison Control Centers, at least 100,000 U.S. farmworkers are treated annually for pesticide-related illness. According to the World Resources Institute, nearly 313,000 farmworkers suffer from pesticide-related illnesses each year internationally, and as many as 1,000 die.

In California, thirty-four farmworkers became ill after reentering a cotton field that had recently been sprayed. Thirty of the workers went to the hospital and the other four were treated medically over

*A sign warns farmworkers of recent sprays. Reentering a field too soon may result in pesticide-related illnesses.*

the next week. The problem might have been avoided. The workers entered the field too early after spraying, even though there were posted and oral warnings about when to reenter the field. But, apparently, these warnings were not sufficient protection for the workers. Lack of communication can lead to such a situation. Farmworkers from Mexico may face a language barrier that prevents them from understanding the dangers and precautions needed when handling pesticides.

In developing countries, where people are poor and regulation may be lax, the dangers to farmworkers may be even greater. In the United States, a farmer may ride a tractor that sprays the pesticides downward and behind him on the field. In a country where many farmers cannot afford tractors, the pesticide is sprayed by hand as the applicator walks through the field, a situation that increases exposure to the chemical. If the climate is hot, farmworkers may not wear protective gear.

In developing countries there are also reports that older (and thus perhaps more dangerous) pesticides may be kept in storage. For example, Nepal, according to a U.S. pesticide management specialist who inspected warehouses there in 1997, is storing more than seventy-five tons of obsolete pesticides throughout the country, some in open, leaking containers.

## Conclusion

Pesticides can cause both acute and chronic harm. Chronic harm appears to arouse the greatest concern, especially the possibility of harm to children. A 1993 study warning that children may be more sensitive to pesticides they inhale or ingest has led to tighter government regulation in the United States. Evidence exists that many claims about pesticides are exaggerated, but clearly some people are at greater risk of exposure than others. These include farmworkers and people who live in agricultural communities, in the United States and around the world.

# CHAPTER 3

# Pesticides and Agriculture

If pesticides put the environment and humans at risk for potential adverse effects, then why are they so widely used? The answer, of course, is that they provide benefits.

Perhaps most important, pesticides are a critical factor in ensuring a bountiful food supply. They have become an integral part of the world's system of food production. Although that may not always be the case in the future, more people would go hungry today without pesticides to increase the food supply.

In a book on pesticide policy, Christopher J. Bosso attempts to explain to his readers how modern pesticides changed agriculture. "Most Americans today are several steps removed from the farm, and food is something to be purchased in prepackaged form in super-markets, not something to be wrested from nature," he writes. "Few urbanites can picture the devastation wrought on wheat crops by stem rust, on corn by the corn borer, on cotton by the boll weevil, or on livestock by scabies or cholera." For farmers back then, such pests were "costly banes."[31] Pesticides offered a way to stop these scourges.

## The Green Revolution

It would be negligent to talk about world food production without a discussion of what has come to be known as the Green Revolution. This refers to advances in technology between 1960 and 1990 that greatly increased the ability of farmers around the world to produce food.

*Norman E. Borlaug (left) and a farmworker stand in a hybrid wheat field grown with Borlaug's miracle seeds.*

The major innovation of this era was the development of "miracle seeds," new hybrids (that is, new varieties made by crossbreeding different kinds of seeds) that could produce much larger amounts of grain per acre. So, using the same amount of land and effort, farmers could produce much more food.

The key research team behind these miracle seeds worked in Mexico in the mid-1940s and included American plant breeder Norman E. Borlaug, who later won the Nobel Peace Prize for his work. The improved seeds boosted Mexican wheat production and helped avert famine in India and Pakistan. Corn and rice seeds followed the wheat varieties. A network of research centers was started, mainly in developing countries, spreading the new seeds into countries like China, Malaysia, and the Philippines.

The results of the Green Revolution were dramatic. According to the Food and Agriculture Organization, between 1961 and 1998 average cereal yields (that is, the amount of grain produced per acre) went up by 126 percent. "As a result," writes one authority, "average daily food suplies per person increased 24 percent globally from 1961–1998...."[32]

Another illustration of the tremendous increase in food production is the change in bushels of corn per acre harvested in the United States. In 1900, American farmers produced about 28 bushels of corn per acre. In 1950, the figure was 38 bushels per acre. By 2000, farmers were growing 140 bushels of corn per acre, an astounding increase. "In the half century from 1950 to 2000, total agricultural productivity more than doubled," says one author. [33]

The Green Revolution did not wipe out hunger and malnutrition, but it cut them back enormously. In the early 1960s, world food supplies were sufficient to supply 2,255 calories per person per day. In 1998, that figure was 2,792. In developing countries, 35 percent of the population was continually underfed in 1970; today that figure is 19 percent.

While miracle seeds were at the heart of the Green Revolution, other technologies also contributed to the increase in crop production. These included new ways to store and handle foods, better irrigation, more efficient transportation and distribution (resulting in less food spoilage), as well as fertilizers and pesticides.

To convey an idea of the agricultural benefits that come from pesticides, Indur M. Goklany offers some figures. At present, he says, 42 percent of all the crops in the field never reach the consumer. Although some of this loss is due to waste or spoilage, much of it comes from insects and other pests that kill the crops in the field or in storage or transportation. Yet without pesticides and other means of controlling pests, the figure would be 70 percent. Thus, around the world, pesticides are a key element in agricultural production.

## Other Benefits

The benefits of pesticides are not just production of more food, although that is critical. They also allow foods to be produced at a lower cost, making healthful foods available to more people. This leads to better nutrition and longer lives.

"Pesticides are used widely in agriculture in the United States," wrote the National Research Council in its 1993 report on pesticides in children's diets. "Their application has improved crop yields and increased the quantity of fresh fruits and vegetables in the diet, thereby contributing to improvements in public health." [34] So even a report that recommended tighter regulations of pesticide residues for children's sake recognized the value of pesticides. Furthermore, as indicated in chapter 2, eating more fruits and vegetables may even reduce cancers.

Another role for pesticides is to kill mycotoxins. These are the dangerous mold residues that can grow in seeds, grains, nuts, and spices that have been stored in warehouses. One example is aflatoxin, which is associated with cancer of the liver, and is found in moldy corn, peanuts, and cottonseed. Outbreaks of disease from mycotoxins are rare in developed countries, but between 1974 and 1975, one hundred people living in India died from eating moldy corn. In Ethiopia, in 1978, people died and lost limbs from eating food contaminated with fungal alkaloids.

Insecticides became a powerful weapon in the 1960s in fighting plagues of locusts, the swarming insects that have attacked agriculture since biblical times. Today, spray programs are still used for locust emergencies. One such emergency occurred in 1997 in Madagascar, an island off the east coast of Africa with a population of 15 million, mainly farmers. When a plague of locusts hit the island, the European Commission donated funds to support aerial spraying of fipronil. Although the program wiped out the locusts that year, the action was criticized. The island is known for its biodiversity and contains species found nowhere else in the world. Some critics said there was inade-

*Without insecticide control, swarms of locusts can devastate crops.*

*Pesticides used can often seep into the ground so that they contaminate the soil and are washed by rain into streams.*

quate environmental monitoring, the spraying went on too long, and the chemicals were unnecessarily toxic.

## Environmental Impacts

Pesticides used in crop production can cause environmental damage. It was, of course, damage to wildlife from DDT and other pesticides that led to the 1972 ban on DDT in the United States. Nearly thirty years later, awareness of the impact of DDT on bird populations remains high among international and national environmental organizations, with a number of groups calling for a global ban on DDT and other pesticides.

Pesticides can drift from fields, and rain can wash them into streams and soil. They can enter the food supply of fish and other wildlife. According to an extensive survey article by Cornell biologist David Pimentel and others, an estimated 6 million to 14 million fish die from pesticides out of a total of 141 million that are killed annually. Each year, several thousand domestic animals in the United States, including livestock and pets, are poisoned by pesticides. Most farm pesticides are toxic to bees, which pollinate fruit and vegetables. One bee expert estimates that 20 percent of all losses of honeybee colonies are from pesticide exposure.

Pimentel and his associates attempted to quantify all the effects of pesticide use, including those on the environment and human health, and to compare them with the estimated benefits of pesticide use. The authors included costs of pesticides that are usually ignored. For example, they attempted to quantify the medical care for people injured or killed by pesticides; the loss of livestock hurt by pesticides; crop loss due to the destruction of natural predators and pests that develop resistance; and the cost of lower honeybee populations and fish killed by the pesticides. The researchers also assigned a dollar value to the birds that were harmed and included the amount of money being spent to save species that had been endangered by pesticides, as well as the cost to restore or substitute for contaminated surface and groundwater. They included the cost of federal and state government programs that train and register pesticide applicators, register pesticides, and monitor and control pesticide pollution.

Using these figures, Pimentel and his associates estimated the total costs—costs that are usually ignored—of pesticides in the United States to be $8.123 billion a year. Only $3 billion, they said, were paid for by the farmers who purchased the pesticides. Society paid the rest. The authors also contend that the full environmental costs are probably larger. Left out were the costs of accidental poisonings, harm to livestock, pets, wild animals, and plants, and unrecorded losses of fish and wildlife and of crops, trees, and other plants, as well as unknown costs from harm to humans such as cancer and sterility.

However, several experts have pointed out an environmental *benefit* from use of pesticides and fertilizers. Higher yields mean that more food can be produced on smaller amounts of land. Indur M. Goklany agrees that fertilizer and pesticide runoff into rivers and streams may threaten fish and birds, but doubts that it will lead to the silent spring feared by Rachel Carson. "Paradoxically," he says, "agricultural technology is also responsible for forestalling any silent springs, at least so far." If technology had stayed at the level of 1961, he figures, "producing as much food as was actually produced in 1998 would have required more than a doubling of land devoted to agriculture." He estimates that "an additional area the size of South

America minus Chile would have to be plowed under." [35] Most of that land today may be open space that allows a diverse array of plants and wild animals to thrive.

# Changes in Agriculture

In addition to environmental impacts, other concerns are sometimes expressed about the agricultural technology that accompanied the Green Revolution. New technology has spurred a shift in farming. Traditional subsistence farming, in which a household produces most of its own food, has been replaced by farms devoted to single crops. Farmers increasingly produce a single cash crop, which they sell for money. They use the money to buy food and other products for their families.

Some people argue that this has led to large "superfarms," and that these have squeezed out the small family farms because they cannot compete. When the economy takes a dive, small operators have the least ability to sell their crops at lower prices, so they are the ones who are hurt. Thus, the massive changes in agricultural technology, of which pesticide use is a part, have social effects that ripple throughout developing countries.

This may be true, but the decline in the number of people in agriculture is a trend that has occurred in every developed nation and is likely to continue. People have left farms and moved to cities. At the turn of this century, about 40 percent of the U.S. population either had farms or did farm work. Today, only 2 percent of Americans farm commercially (others may have "hobby farms" or grow vegetable gardens). There were 32 million farmers in the United States in 1920, whereas there are 4.6 million today. Small farmers have not always been replaced by superfarms, however. Family farms do remain, although they are generally much larger and more efficient than they were in 1920.

Other complaints are that the Green Revolution has created monoculture agriculture—the production of a single crop in fields that stretch for many acres and are heavily dependent on chemicals. Corn, for instance, is a nitrogen-intensive plant. If corn is grown year after year on the same land, nitrogen must be put back in the soil through chemical fertilizers. If the corn is grown along with or alternating with legumes (beans and related plants that restore nitrogen

*Farmers rely on chemicals to restore nutrients in the soil as they are depleted by crops such as corn.*

naturally), nitrogen can be maintained without chemicals, or with the use of fewer chemicals, some argue. Many of these chemicals are petrochemicals, derived from petroleum. One environmental group says that "as the new seeds spread, petrochemicals become part of farming."[36]

Some argue that reliance on pesticides has led to a vicious circle popularly known as the pesticides treadmill. As pests become resistant to the poisons, ever greater amounts of pesticides are needed to get rid of the pests. Barbara Dinham, writing in a United Nations publication, says that "insects can quickly develop resistance to the chemicals. Pests then tend to increase rapidly, encouraging even greater pesticide use, which again is likely to be ineffective."[37] Although this may occur, there is evidence that pesticide use has leveled off, possibly as new techniques are adopted that lessen this treadmill. The EPA confirms that annual use of herbicides is lower than it was in 1980, and the Associated Press reported in October 2001 that pesticide use in California is at the lowest level since 1992. An official of the American Farm Bureau Federation, a farmers' organization, says that high pesticide prices have spurred farmers to cut back.

Many environmental groups such as the World Wildlife Fund have been outspoken in their opposition to pesticides. Yet at present pesticides are critical to the world's system of food production. Buffeted by conflicting pressures, the United Nations is divided within itself. The United Nations Environment Programme (UNEP) is pushing for a reduction in pesticide use, while the Food and Agriculture Organization (FAO) is attempting to reduce hunger through increasing crop yields, and it considers pesticides as part of that effort. At the World Food Summit in 1996, the FAO estimated that 800 million people today experience serious hunger. The organization set a goal of reducing this number to 400 million by 2015.

In its public statements, the FAO attempts to find a middle way. It supports "effective prevention and progressive control of plant and animal pests and diseases" and "regional collaboration in plant pests and animal disease control and the widespread development and use of integrated pest management practices."[38] These statements imply that pesticides will continue to be used but suggest that their importance should be reduced.

## Organic Farming

Concern about pesticides has sparked interest in alternative farming techniques, especially organic farming. This refers to growing crops with few synthetic pesticides or fertilizers and raising livestock that are free from most synthetic pesticides, growth hormones, and antibiotics. There has been an organic farming business for many years, even as far back as the 1950s in the United States, but it has received greater attention in the past decade.

Hervé la Prairie is president of the International Federation of Organic Agriculture Movements (IFOAM), an organization that promotes organic farming worldwide. La Prairie contends that organic farming "provides high yields, is environmentally accountable and is sustainable in the true sense of the word."[39]

Yet whether this optimistic view of organic farming proves to be accurate remains to be seen. On the one hand, chemical-free farming is growing rapidly—by 10 percent per year in Austria and 7.8 percent in Switzerland. Countries like the United States, France, and Japan, are experiencing annual growth rates that exceed 20 percent. At the same time, organic food remains a niche market; that is, it has a limited customer base.

Although there are exceptions, the cost of organic food tends to be higher than that of food grown with synthetic fertilizers and pesticides.

For example, in 2001, visits to grocery stores in two Massachusetts towns, Fitchburg and Lunenburg, found that nearly all organic produce examined was more expensive than traditional or nonorganic produce. The same was true at a Los Alamos, New Mexico, grocery store. However, at a Wal-Mart supermarket in New Mexico, organic carrots and nonorganic were priced nearly the same; organic spinach was about 200 percent higher.

In some cases, organically grown produce looks less attractive, and this too diminishes its appeal. For decades, the agriculture industry has strived to make apple skins as uniform in color as possible, tomatoes as round as possible, and squashes and cucumbers consistent in shape. Many people still want these characteristics, which are not always available with organically grown food.

As time has passed, farmers have been able to obtain certification that they are farming organically. This is important to many consumers of organic foods, who want to be sure that the produce they are buying is free of synthetic chemicals. Certification is formal approval that an organic farm has met certain standards. It can be governmental or private, as long as there is a consistent set of standards and a method for monitoring to ensure that the grower has met the standards.

Certification varies from country to country. In the United States, a federal law sets production and handling standards for organic

## Organic Versus Nonorganic
### The Price of Produce

| PRODUCE | ORGANIC | NONORGANIC |
|---|---|---|
| Carrots (per lb.) | .99 | .50 |
| Potatoes (per 5 lb. bag) | 3.99 | From 2.50 to 3.49 |
| Cherry tomatoes (per ounce) | .29 | .22 |
| Celery hearts (per lb.) | 1.80 | .45 |
| Onions (per lb.) | 1.95 | .47 |
| Cauliflower (per lb.) | 1.59 | .99 |
| Green bell peppers (ea.) | .99 | .69 |

Produce from Smith's, Los Alamos, NM, November 2001.

*Organic farmers find alternatives to pesticides when battling crop pests and their larvae.*

foods. Anyone selling more than $5,000 worth of products must be certified by an agent accredited by the U.S. Department of Agriculture. Without that accreditation it cannot advertise its foods as organically produced.

Worries about chemical additives and, more recently, risks such as mad cow disease may continue to increase the appeal of organic farming. Mad cow disease is believed to be spread when cattle are fed protein meal supplements that have remnants of other animals contaminated with the disease. Cattle on an organic farm would be free range, meaning that for the most part they would graze freely or be fed hay.

Whether there is a place for organic farming in poorer countries is another question. Dennis Avery doesn't think so. An expert on international agriculture, he has written a book whose title makes his position clear, *Saving the Planet with Pesticides and Plastic*. Avery contends that stopping the use of pesticides will reverse much of the progress of the Green Revolution because the yields from pesticide-free crops are lower than those that use them.

"The day may come when we'll understand biology and ecology well enough at the level of cells and molecules to make organic farming a high-yield success," he says. "But that in-depth knowledge is at least decades away." Now, he says, organic farming produces "far lower" and "far more erratic yields"[40] for many crops.

Yields tend to be erratic because farmers must keep changing crops each year. If they don't, the crops will gradually deplete the nutrients in the soil. According to Avery, mainstream farmers can keep growing corn each year, but an organic farmer may get a corn crop only once every three years.

Robert Quinn, an organic farmer in Montana, disagrees with this pessimistic viewpoint, at least with wheat, which he grows on his farm. He says that after a three- or four-year transition period, there is very little difference in overall yields between his farm and his neighbors'. "In very wet years, we do see significantly lower yields compared to our neighbors because of their high inputs [of fertilizers and pesticides]," he says. "In an average year, however, our yields are about the same as our neighbors, and in very dry years we normally harvest more."[41]

At the same time, Quinn recognizes that organic farming is not simple, even in the United States, where there is a good payoff because some consumers are willing to pay more for organic products. He says that most farmers need to take five to six years to make the conversion from traditional agriculture to organic. Before he changed his farm from traditional agriculture to organic, he conducted a lot of research. He wanted to be sure that there was significant demand for organic foods and that they could be sold for a premium (that is, a higher) price. Helping him win customers was his unusual product, a wheat strain that originated in Egypt. He was able to market it as a distinctive brand.

# Conclusion

Pesticides play a large and positive role in today's world food supply. They contribute to a system of agriculture that has increased food production per acre dramatically over the past few decades.

At the same time, there are costs. Pesticides can build up in the soil and run off into streams, where they are ingested by fish and other wildlife. Some people claim that farmers enter a pesticides treadmill.

The debates over pesticides have led to many changes in their use, from greater regulation to new techniques. Although pesticides will be part of agriculture's near future, their use will undoubtedly change in the years ahead.

# CHAPTER 4

# Pesticides and Disease

**M**alaria is one of the world's worst killers. It infects between 300 and 500 million people a year, killing more than 1 million, many of them children. Malaria is a parasite that is carried by mosquitoes from one person to another. Pesticides have a role in combating malaria, as well as other deadly mosquito-borne diseases such as dengue fever.

Yet controversy surrounds the application of insecticides to fight disease. The weapon that seems to be the most effective against malaria is DDT, which many people consider to be so environmentally harmful that it should not be used.

Thus, environmentalists who oppose the use of DDT are pitted against public health officials in a grim dispute. Janet Raloff, a science reporter, summarizes the issue this way: "Though environmentalists have come to demand this poison's elimination from the face of the earth, some tropical-disease specialists laud DDT as an irreplaceable weapon in their fight against malaria. Which view prevails may be a life-and-death matter for nearly a half-billion people."[42]

## Malaria

In addition to killing many of its victims, malaria disables others. Malaria parasites "have a voracious appetite," says one observer, "and in just a few hours can suck as much as a quarter pound of hemoglobin out of the red blood cells of an infected human being."[43]

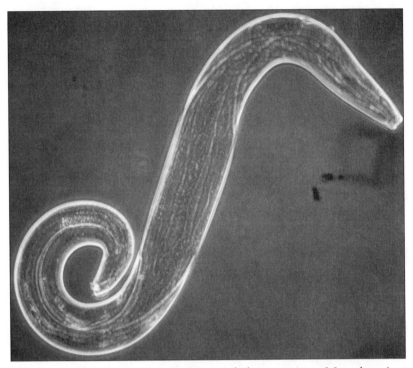

*The malaria parasite is transmitted to people by mosquitoes. More than 1 million people die from malaria each year.*

Those who survive malaria often suffer chronic symptoms of the disease. Their ability to ward off other diseases is weakened, and many suffer from continuing anemia.

"Despite massive efforts to eradicate the disease in the 1950s and early 1960s, there is more human malaria in the world today than at any other time in history,"[44] write two specialists in tropical illnesses. One-quarter of the world's population is at risk of catching malaria.

Public health officials have been trying to eradicate malaria for a century, by draining swamps where mosquitoes thrive and spraying areas with pesticides. Success has been spotty. Although malaria has been essentially wiped out in Europe and North America, it remains widespread in other parts of the world, especially the tropics and subtropics. Most who die from it are in Africa, but it does not exist only in Third World countries. Because of international travel, in the United States, approximately one thousand cases are reported each year, writes Ellen Ruppel Shell in the *Atlantic Monthly,* and it can be found in more than half the countries in the world. Ominously, malaria is reemerging in places where it was previously under control or even eradicated, like North Africa, Southeast and Central Asia, South America, and the Caribbean.

There are two main ways to attack the disease. One is vector control—getting rid of the mosquitoes (the vector) that carry it. This can be done with insecticides or by destroying the insect's breeding grounds. In the 1930s, the U.S. government dealt aggressively with malaria by draining millions of acres of swamp. Similarly, removing forests and jungle to get rid of the shade and moisture that allow mosquitoes to thrive can combat malaria.

The other strategy is to use antimalarial drugs to fight the parasites, both before and after infection. Most common is chloroquine (a form of quinine, a medicine made from the bark of a cinchona tree). There is no vaccine to prevent infection; chloroquine only moderates the effects of the disease; it is not a cure.

Most experts agree that the cheapest and most effective weapon has been DDT, although even at the height of its use DDT never completely eliminated malaria. In 1944, the U.S. military introduced DDT to control malaria. By fighting lice-borne typhus it saved thousands of soldiers' lives. This led to its widespread use around the world. At the same time, the military introduced antimalarial drugs such as chloroquine.

In 1955, recognizing the promise of DDT, the World Health Organization (WHO), United Nations Children's Emergency Fund (UNICEF), and the Food and Agriculture Organization (FAO) began the Global Malaria Eradication Campaign. The program had two major thrusts: to spray DDT on the interior of homes to kill mosquitoes, and to identify infection early and treat it with antimalarial drugs.

The hope was that malaria could be completely eradicated in most of the world. (In sub-Saharan Africa, where insufficient health care and poor transport infrastructure made eradication impossible, the goal was merely to control the disease.) "Malaria rates went down, and hopes for public health soared,"[45] writes one reporter.

Complete and swift eradication where possible was crucial because by the early 1950s it had become clear that the disease-bearing mosquitoes could build up resistance to DDT. The aim of the program was to wipe out the mosquitoes before they had a chance to become resistant. But many countries did not have the money or the infrastructure to keep the programs going consistently. For example, successful spraying programs needed detailed maps of the malarial areas so that sprayers could target the highest risk areas, but not every city or country had such maps. A country also needed a reasonable health care system to monitor the disease, and such hospitals and public health personnel were few in many places.

Some mosquitoes survived and reproduced, creating populations of insecticide-resistant mosquitoes. Insufficient application, rather than excessive use, appears to have led to resistance by insects, but the exact causes of resistance are not fully understood. The theory is that if insecticides are applied in sublethal doses, survivors will remain. If they breed, then there will be more resistant insects in the next generation, and so on. A different theory, however, also has been offered: The insects may simply learn to avoid the insecticides.

DDT proved to be very effective in controlling mosquitoes where the numbers of malaria infections were moderate, as in Europe, North America, and Egypt. There were some success stories in other places too, even where the number of malaria victims initially seemed out of control. India brought an estimated number of 75 million cases in 1951 down to 50,000 in 1961.

Perhaps the best known DDT success story took place in Sri Lanka where spraying began in 1946. Ten years of spraying brought the number of cases from 3 million down to 7,300 and had eliminated all deaths due to the disease. By the 1960s, there was only a handful of cases.

These apparent successes were short-lived, however. Harold Varmus, who works for the National Institutes of Health, said that he saw "almost no malaria" when he worked in India in 1966. When he returned in 1988 he found a "raging epidemic."[46]

In some countries, after spraying had gone on for some years, it looked as though the disease was under control, so some governments stopped malaria control efforts. The disease returned full force. Sri Lanka, the country that had so much success, had only seventeen recorded cases of malaria in 1963, but by 1969 the number surged to more than half a million. In regions of Colombia and Peru, the risk of malaria doubled when spraying ceased in the 1990s.

Some countries stopped spraying because it was costly and the disease seemed under control, but pressure from Western countries also discouraged the use of DDT. Donors of aid, government agencies such as the U.S. Agency for International Development as well

*DDT spraying in mosquito breeding areas has helped reduce the number of malaria cases.*

as private groups, wanted reliance on DDT to stop. Thus, only twenty-three countries currently use the chemical to control mosquitoes and the diseases they carry, and very few countries produce the chemical.

Other nations are torn between using DDT and following the wishes of wealthier nations. These include Belize and Bolivia. At the 1999 annual meeting of the American Association for the Advancement of Science, Jorge A. Planco of the Ministry of Health in Belize reported that malaria had been nearly eradicated in the 1960s, primarily because people sprayed their homes with DDT. In the 1980s, the government began to phase out DDT, and the number of malaria cases started to rise. In 1999, the country resumed spraying with an alternative insecticide. Because alternative pesticides are much more expensive, Planco said that the cost of pesticides is using up 90 percent of the budget for malaria control. This has left little money for treatment, surveillance, and control of breeding grounds.

Struggles and debates over whether to use DDT continue. South Africa, responding to pressure from environmentalists, abandoned DDT in favor of more expensive insecticides in 1996. Within three years, mosquitoes resistant to the replacement invaded KwaZulu-Natal province, where they had not been seen since DDT spraying began in the 1940s. Malaria cases soared from 4,117 cases in 1995 to 27,238 cases in 1999. Other provinces experienced similar catastrophes. The government of South Africa returned to using DDT.

In addition to its lower cost, an advantage of DDT is that mosquitoes will not enter a house that has been sprayed with it. This was illustrated in a recent study. Scientists in Belize compared three huts. One was sprayed with DDT, one with deltamethrin, an insecticide that is considered one of the best alternatives to DDT, and one was untreated. Only 3 percent as many mosquitoes even entered the DDT-sprayed hut as entered the other two. This indicates that DDT not only kills mosquitoes but also repels them.

In Mozambique, the use of DDT ended several decades ago. Eighty percent of the country's health budget came from donor funds, and donors refused to allow the use of DDT, according to an article in the *British Medical Journal*. Mozambique is an extremely poor country, with an average annual income of $220. After the floods of 2000, the country became a prolific breeding ground for mosquitoes, but DDT spraying was not available. According to the World Food Program, tens of thousands of people contracted malaria directly after the flood because of mosquitoes breeding in the floodwaters. The United Nations lists malaria as the number one cause of death in Mozambique.

The tragic spread of malaria also had other consequences in Mozambique. A group of companies working with the Mozambican government were building a $1.34 billion aluminum smelter plant, one of the nation's largest industrial projects. So many of the foreign staff helping to build the plant contracted malaria (and several died) that the companies refused to send replacements until the malaria was brought under control. A spraying program was implemented, but the additional costs (including malaria testing) led the developers to decide not to expand the project.

# The Current Debate

In the late 1990s, the United Nations Environmental Programme (UNEP) began discussion of a global treaty that would ban a list of chemicals called the "dirty dozen" worldwide. On the list are pesticides such as dieldrin, aldrin, and other persistent organic pollutants (POPs). DDT is on the list. The World Wildlife Fund (WWF), a leading international environmental group, campaigned in 1999 for the treaty to include a target date, 2007, for worldwide elimination of DDT. The intent was to set a deadline that would force the scientific community to develop options for less toxic malaria control. "DDT is such a potent chemical that as long as it is used anywhere in the world, nobody is safe," says Clifton Curtis, director of the World Wildlife Fund's Global Toxics Initiative. "There is no longer a question about whether DDT should be banned, only how soon it can happen while still ensuring developing countries access to safe, affordable alternative malaria controls,"[47] Curtis says.

The reason for the proposed ban is primarily the one identified by Rachel Carson years ago, that DDT persists in the environment and can cause serious harm to some fish-eating birds if it accumulates in their tissue. Says Sharon Newsome, director of the Environment and Health Program for Physicians for Social Responsibility, "We know that DDT bioaccumulates; it persists in the environment, and it travels widely." She adds, "You may use it in Africa, but it ends up in many, many other places."[48]

Opposing the treaty were tropical disease specialists who believe that DDT is the best way to fight malaria. Three hundred seventy-one doctors, health economists, and scientists signed a letter warning of the consequences if UNEP outlaws DDT and other "dirty dozen" pesticides. They asked that the United Nations continue to allow DDT to be used for house spraying in regions where malaria is a serious problem. In response, WWF dropped its deadline in the negotiations.

"DDT should remain available for focused and controlled use to help nations where the disease remains," contends Harold M. Koenig, former surgeon general of the U.S. Navy. "Banning DDT will cause the gap between rich and poor nations to continue to expand."[49]

*A representative of Canada signs the global treaty that bans the use of chemicals known as the "dirty dozen."*

In the end, 127 nations agreed in 2001 that all twelve chemicals should be banned eventually. Experts believe that within four or five years, production and use of nine of the twelve chemicals will be prohibited. However, a clause allows DDT to be used to combat malaria until a cheaper method is found.

Environmentalists claim that substitutes can be used today to fight malaria. Yet in Ethiopia, where the nearest substitute would be triple the price, Berhane Mikail of the country's health authority, disagrees. "We don't have an alternative," he says. "It's not practical in our situation. It doesn't mate with the reality of this area. We cannot ban these insecticides, because we don't have alternatives."[50]

Even though DDT can still be legally used in some countries, international pressure not to use it has led UNICEF, WHO, and the World Bank to try to create an alternative. A new program, Roll Back Malaria, relies on techniques other than DDT spraying. Launched in 1998, the program has a limited objective: reducing infant mortality by 50 percent. It relies primarily on mosquito nets that have been soaked with pesticides—not DDT, but pyrethroids, which are considered less toxic and less persistent. They may also be less effective. The nets cost between five and ten dollars each and must be continually re-treated.

Other treatments that have found some acceptance and availability include "mosquito coils, repellants and other materials; early detection, containment, and prevention of malaria epidemics; and strengthening of local capacity to monitor malaria in affected regions," says a UNICEF publication.[51]

Yet the substitutes may actually be more harmful than DDT to the people who use them. The pesticides are supposed to be low in toxicity but there is "unprotected skin contact when nets are dipped in tubs of insecticide for retreatment and through exposure to air filtered through the insecticide-impregnated nets."[52] Even so, the International Association of Physicians in AIDS Care supports the Roll Back Malaria program, arguing that the pyrethroids are safe. On its website the association points out that "the chemicals bind tightly to fabric and are resistant to washing with soap and water" and quotes the Roll Back Malaria program as saying it is unlikely that "the accidental licking of the net would pose a health hazard to the child."[53]

But are the newer techniques affordable in areas where average income can be measured in the hundreds rather than the thousands of dollars? David Maguire, project director with the Academy for Educational Development, a company that is trying to make the bed nets available and affordable, admits that family income is small in many of the countries battling malaria. However, he feels that families already spend a significant percentage of income on treatment for malaria. "Once the consumer understands the value of a product, they will pay for it."[54]

In contrast, Richard Tren and Robert Bate claim that not only are the substitutes more expensive, but they are less effective than DDT spraying programs. "Recent research shows that unless the entire community has insecticide-treated bed nets and they are used effectively, they prove ineffective in malaria control."[55]

# A Future for DDT?

The problem of malaria is not going to be easily resolved. However, a view more favorable toward pesticides may be developing in the Western countries. If so, the barriers against using DDT may weaken.

People respond to incentives, and new concern has arisen about a mosquito-borne disease in the United States: West Nile virus. "Until

August 1999," writes medical reporter Jane E. Brody in the *New York Times,* "most city residents found mosquitoes but occasional summertime pests, to be endured perhaps at an evening concert in Central Park. Then came the news that, somehow or other, a native mosquito, *Culex pipiens,* . . . had acquired an exotic virus that could cause a fatal brain infection, West Nile encephalitis."[56]

In 1999, seven people in New York City and nearby counties died of the West Nile virus, and sixty-two cases of severe disease were reported, even with the spraying of malathion, a powerful pesticide. In 2000, New York sprayed with Anvil, a pyrethroid-based pesticide. Twenty-one cases were reported in the New York City area (including parts of New Jersey and Connecticut), and two people died through September.

The virus has been also found in Africa, Europe, the Middle East, west and central Asia, and Oceania. In 1974 an epidemic in South Africa produced tens of thousands of infections. In a rare outbreak in Romania in 1996, there were nearly four hundred serious cases, most of which had acute central-nervous system infections, and seventeen deaths. The number of mild cases could not be estimated.

Previously, Americans had been able to ignore diseases such as malaria. Although cases do turn up, they mostly occur in travelers who pick them up in exotic locations in Africa or Latin America. However, the West Nile virus was an example of a disease that might

*A mosquito sucks blood from a human arm. More than ever, people are fearful of contracting a mosquito-borne disease.*

be taking root in the United States, carried by common, everyday mosquitoes. This new development may lead people to think more broadly about the dangers of pests, and not just the dangers from pesticides.

## Conclusion

As long as malaria is a scourge, and pesticides appear to be the most effective way to control the disease, the controversy over the use of DDT is likely to continue. Spraying continues in some countries in spite of environmentalists' objections. Other methods that use more modern, less powerful pesticides are also being tried. Perhaps a vaccine against malaria will be found, and the need for pesticides will dwindle. But mosquitoes carry other diseases, too. Until modern medicine conquers them all, or scientists create harmless chemicals, pesticides will be used to protect human health—and elicit criticism.

# CHAPTER 5

# The Future of Pesticides

Pesticides are in the middle of a tug-of-war. Because they are poisons, many people don't want them around, yet their value in protecting crops and combating disease cannot be denied. Given this conflict, making precise predictions about pesticide use is difficult, but it is possible to discern some trends. One observer foresees that scientists and pesticide manufacturers will engage in a "persistent quest to design and develop a safer range of pesticides, and evolve new and novel strategies to control insect pests and minimize crop damages."[57]

Clearly, the strong government regulation that took shape in the 1970s in the United States will continue. America is unlikely ever to go back to the days of government-encouraged spraying without limits, or allow pesticides to be invented and marketed without stringent requirements for testing and labeling. The rest of the world is moving in that direction as well. Partly because of this regulation, but also in response to changing public attitudes, pesticides have become safer in the past fifty years.

Second, efforts to reduce pesticide use continue. Farmers are adopting what is often described as integrated pest management, or IPM. This is a collection of techniques that make more effective use of smaller quantities of pesticides.

Third, new technologies to genetically modify foods may do away with traditional pesticides in many places and situations. However, these technologies have their own critics and cannot be viewed as a panacea.

## Different Pesticides

Today's pesticides are different from those in the past. They are less persistent and less toxic to humans. Nevertheless, they are still subject to strict controls, and the Environmental Protection Agency (EPA) continues to consider bans on some of them. For example, parathion, a widely used pesticide, is less toxic to birds and mammals than others but still dangerous to fish. Methyl bromide is currently slated for a ban because it is believed to contribute to depletion of ozone in the stratosphere.

The elimination of methyl bromide by 2005 is probably the biggest regulatory issue that producers face. This chemical is used on soil to control insects, nematodes, weeds, and rodents. Coastal Berry Company is one of two dozen strawberry growers taking part in government-funded trials to find a replacement for methyl bromide. "I think most growers out there to some capacity are trying different alternatives," says David Murray, a Coastal Berry manager. "I think they figure if they wait until the last minutes to find something they're going to miss the boat."[58]

The 1996 Food Quality Protection Act, which required the EPA to set new pesticide standards with special emphasis on children, is

*Although pesticides are still widely used, many growers are working with government agencies to test alternatives.*

also beginning to change regulation. The EPA has started reevaluating the allowed residue levels on foods.

If this leads to the elimination of some pesticides, it could put a squeeze on farmers. According to Michael Fumento, "Prevent them from using any one insecticide and you force them to switch to an inferior one that requires more chemical per acre, increasing the chance of run-off into water supplies. For some crops, there are currently *no* replacements." [59]

Although this is a legitimate worry, it is fair to say that most actions by the EPA have met resistance from agriculture and from chemical producers over many years, yet both have responded with innovation that allows fruits and vegetables to continue to appear in supermarkets. In the 1970s, the EPA began eliminating the use of the powerful pesticides aldrin and dieldrin, and required more testing and more rigid standards of safety for new products. The number of new pesticide products fell from about seven hundred a year to twenty to thirty. Farmers who grew strawberries, onions, and pineapples were alarmed because no replacements for aldrin and dieldrin seemed available for their crops, and producers of crops grown in small quantities were particularly worried that they might not have pesticides available. "You have to concentrate on new pesticides for the bigger markets and hope they'll be useful in other areas," [60] said a research and development manager for a large pesticide company at the time. Apparently, the companies succeeded. Fruits and vegetables continue to be grown in the United States; however, these foods may cost more than they would otherwise.

The United States currently produces 25 percent of all pesticides in the world, including those that are banned here but exported to other countries that allow them. South Africa, for instance, requires farmers to register the pesticides that they use. On the list of qualified chemicals are paraquat, aldicarb, pentachlorophenol, and methyl parathion, which have been banned in other countries, including the United States.

Some environmental groups hope to prohibit the export of these pesticides, claiming that they make their way back into the country via imported produce. However, Jonathan Adler, an expert on environmental law, argues that strict U.S. laws on pesticide residues make it unlikely that they can enter. Furthermore, without these pesticides exported from the United States, Third World farmers might use even more toxic chemicals.

*A scientist checks plants for beneficial insects that eliminate pests without the use of chemicals.*

## Reduced-Risk Pesticides

Responding to the concern that usable pesticides are dwindling, the EPA's Office of Pesticide Programs created the Reduced-Risk Pesticides Initiative. The idea is that some that appear to be less dangerous can be reviewed quickly and reach the market sooner. In 1996, the average review time for new products was about three years. Reduced-risk pesticides can be reviewed in about a year.

Included in the reduced-risk category are biopesticides, substances based on natural materials, including plants, bacteria, and certain minerals. Such "natural" substances are not new to the pesticide industry. At the end of 1998, approximately 175 biopesticide ingredients were registered for use in the United States.

One of the best known biopesticides is *Bacillus thuringiensis* (Bt), which has been used in agriculture for about twenty-five years. This is a natural bacterium, harmless to humans, birds, fish, and other vertebrates. When consumed by insect larvae, it causes a loss of appetite, and the larvae don't eat enough to survive. Bt was discovered more than ninety years ago in Japan, where it had infected silkworms. Now it is the most widely used natural pesticide in the world.

Other natural pesticides are compounds from plants that can kill insects. These include nicotine found in tobacco and pyrethroids from the periwinkle plant. Many farmers today use natural pesticides, with chemicals as a backup.

Natural pesticides and other new formulations still pose many of the same problems that chemical pesticides pose. They can kill non-targeted species, including a beneficial species that helps control the pest. When one pest is eliminated, new ones may take over because the competition is gone. And natural pesticides, too, can build up resistance in the insects they attack. Natural pesticides are not necessarily safer than synthetic—they are simply natural poisons.

## Pest Management Programs

Hundreds of years ago, when chemical pesticides were rare or nonexistent, farmers protected their crops through changes in growing practices and other actions. For example, they rotated their crops, so that a pest that fed on one crop would go hungry the next year when another was planted. They destroyed crop refuse and diseased plants to prevent the spread of blights or fungi. They adjusted the timing and location of planting to avoid pests, and even removed pests from stems and stalks by hand.

Many of these techniques are incorporated into what is known as integrated pest management, or IPM. The movement toward IPM took shape in the 1970s, partly in response to Rachel Carson's book, *Silent Spring*, and the growth of the environmental movement. Today this approach to agriculture is used all over the world. It "relies heavily on natural mortality factors such as natural enemies and weather and seeks out control tactics that disrupt these factors as little as possible,"[61] say Mary Louise Flint and Robert van den Bosch, authors of a book on the subject.

IPM aims at relying less on chemicals and more on preventive measures. In addition to physical or cultivation controls, it includes biological controls—the use of natural bacteria or insects to combat harmful ones. For instance, because ladybugs eat aphids and other pests, the USDA's Forest Service uses ladybugs to kill off pine beetles.

An example of physical control is a barrier strip of netting around a crop to keep out birds, bats, and rodents. Another is reducing plant pests by hand-pulling unwanted plants. Other IPM techniques include bug zappers (devices that electrocute insects), spraying crops with soapy water, and vacuuming bugs off vegetation.

Research is also being conducted on pheromones, which are chemicals that attract pests. Some are naturally produced by insects; others are synthesized in a laboratory. In California, pear growers are using "puffers," devices that emit pheromones that smell like female codling moths. The scent attracts male moths, who become confused when they can't find the female, and this disrupts mating behavior. Research on fruit grown with puffers has indicated that only one-tenth of the fruit appears to be damaged by moths; without the puffers, says Rachel Elkins of the University of California at Davis, damage can reach 70 percent. Pheromone puffers have replaced a large portion of the pesticides previously used on pears, Elkins says.

IPM is something of an art. Traditional pesticide application occurs "automatically according to a predetermined schedule," say Flint and van den Bosch, but IPM programs "evolve."[62] The procedures must change with the seasons and as pests and their natural predators come and go.

Because so much judgment and variation are involved, constant monitoring is essential. "Monitoring is a regular, systematic observation of the areas where pest problems might occur, and is a key component in every IPM program," says Karen Delahaut, University of

*Ladybugs are a natural alternative to spraying pesticides because they eat aphids and other pests.*

Wisconsin IPM outreach specialist. "Monitoring isn't just making casual observations while you are in the field doing something else."[63]

Such monitoring can make IPM work. For example, a World Wildlife Fund study found that a collaborative effort among governments, academic institutions, growers, and processors reduced pesticide spraying on potato fields in Wisconsin. These farmers use a computer-based system that keeps track of soil temperature, plant age, humidity, and growth patterns of insects. With this information, pesticides can be applied only when needed. Now the farmers are able to use the same crops for a longer time before rotating them, and soil quality has improved. According to the report, the farmers saved almost $6 million on pesticides and irrigation.

IPM is used in developing countries as well. In the Philippines, where rice is the main crop, the use of pesticides increased steadily from the late 1970s to the mid-1980s but decreased in the early 1990s when IPM was introduced. After farmers were trained in the techniques, they raised rice yields by between 4 percent and 37.5 percent. Yet the expenses of the farmers decreased because they spent less on pesticides.

Clearly, IPM has costs. Monitoring takes time and personnel, training may be required, and farmers must be able to adjust as new pests appear and other problems occur. Agricultural expert Dennis Avery supports the technique; however, he says that IPM "is not a way to replace pesticides, but rather a way to make them more effective."[64]

# A Second Green Revolution?

The Green Revolution, which began to have an impact about thirty years ago, did not cure world hunger, but it dramatically improved food production. In the next thirty years, world population is expected to keep increasing. World population now exceeds 6.1 billion, and according to the United Nations, which projects population figures, it will reach 9.3 billion by 2050. Of this total, more than 8 billion (more people than are on the planet today) will live in what the United Nations calls the less developed regions of the world.

To meet the challenges of this population increase—as well as the increasing desire for better food by people whose incomes are rising—organizations from the World Bank to the Rockefeller Foundation are hoping for a second Green Revolution built around genetically mod-

*Scientists are looking beyond creating hybrids to genetically modifying plant species.*

ified crops. Writing in a supplement to *Nature* magazine, Gordon Conway and Gary Toenniessen say, "In effect, we require a 'Doubly Green Revolution,' an agricultural revolution that is both more productive and more 'green' in terms of conserving natural resources and the environment than the first." One key to such a revolution, they say, is "the application of modern biotechnology directed towards the needs of the poor in developing countries."[65]

Genetically engineered or genetically modified seeds are a new form of plant breeding, which has gone on for centuries. In the past, farmers and scientists created hybrid seeds that had some of the best characteristics of different types of plants. The corn and wheat of the first Green Revolution were hybrids. But genetic engineering goes a step further. The information about the plant's development that is encoded in a gene is transferred from one species to another.

These high-tech transfers allow plant breeders to insert traits that may not exist within the species of plant, or even within a species that could be crossbred with the plant. For instance, genes from another organism can be inserted into the cell of a tomato seed to give it a longer shelf life or to allow the tomato to ripen more slowly than it would without the genes. Other crops may be modified to provide frost resistance.

Genetically engineered crops began to be sold commercially in the United States in 1994. Today, more than three thousand varieties have been developed, tested, and sold in U.S. supermarkets. About one-third of the nation's corn crops are sown with genetically modified seeds, as are about half of the nation's soybeans.

More than 90 percent of these crops are grown in the developed world. This demand will change, however. According to food expert Michael Lipton, China has substantial areas under genetically modified corn, rice, and cotton, and Argentina and Brazil have started to use the seeds.

Crops can be modified to resist pests, so one impact is likely to be lower pesticide use and perhaps, as a result, a decrease in overall agricultural costs. For example, some corn has been modified to include the gene for Bt, the naturally occurring bacterium that kills pests such as the corn borer. Crops with Bt require less pesticide because the pesticide exists within the plant itself.

Another technique is to modify crops so that they resist the extremely strong herbicides that are often sprayed on fields to destroy weeds. If farmers use very strong chemicals, they risk killing the crop in the process, so they have to apply weaker chemicals more often. If the desired plants are, instead, resistant to the herbicide, applications can be stronger and fewer applications will be needed. For example, a genetically modified soybean is resistant to a strong herbicide called Roundup7, which would damage a regular soybean crop but can be used safely around the modified soybeans.

Proponents of genetically modified seeds claim substantial health benefits for them. Already, genes have been inserted into rice to increase its production of beta-carotene, a substance that is converted to vitamin A in the body and protects against blindness. Until now, vitamin A, critical for human health, has been inadequate in the diets of poor people who rely on traditional rice as a food staple. Genetic modification has also increased the level of iron in rice. According to Indur M. Goklany, when these strains are crossbred, the result is especially valuable. "Such rice would help reduce vitamin A and iron deficiency-related deaths and diseases in the developing world,"[66] Goklany writes.

## Opposing Genetic Modification

Genetically modified crops, sometimes called genetically modified organisms (or GMOs), have their critics. Some have conducted protest

*Activists opposed to genetically modified crops (organisms) protest at the site of a biotech conference.*

demonstrations, pressuring companies and regulators in the United States and Europe to stop using the seeds. In one notorious incident, protesters dumped genetically modified soybeans in front of the British prime minister's home. Others vandalized fields where such seeds were being grown. These protests have slowed down the expansion of such crops. One corn chip maker announced that it will not purchase genetically modified corn, and a leading producer of baby foods announced that it will avoid grains that have been genetically manipulated.

As with many new technologies, some objections may reflect fear of the unknown rather than specific problems. Even so, a number of environmental concerns have been raised.

One is that target pests may more quickly develop resistance to crops that have these internal pesticides. The reason is that pesticides such as Bt in modified corn are present all the time, rather than applied periodically.

Another criticism is that nontarget species may be hurt—a charge leveled against most pesticides, whether natural, chemical, or genetically modified. In theory at least, pollen from corn with Bt could drift away from the field where the corn is growing and affect other organisms. A laboratory test reported in the journal *Nature* found that the larvae of monarch butterflies fed with large quantities of Bt-carrying pollen had a high mortality rate. Whether similar effects would occur outside the laboratory—with pollen drifting from an actual cornfield—isn't known, however.

Another worry is that genes from modified crops might enter into genetically similar wild plants. Wild plants that accidentally pick up resistance to herbicides might become "superweeds" that would resist eradication.

Indur M. Goklany points out that there are ways to address most of these problems. Although it is possible that weeds could pick up resistance to herbicides, he points out that "farmers have a substantial incentive for preventing weeds from acquiring herbicide tolerance and, if that fails, to keep such weeds in check."[67] Jonathan Adler, commenting on the criticisms, also observes that the risks, while "conceivable," are "not particularly unique"[68] to modified organisms.

Blake Hurst, a writer and a farmer, says that he and other farmers are puzzled about all the protests. "Genetic modification allows us to cut our use of manmade chemicals as we tend our crops,"[69] he says. A survey of corn producers in six states in the United States found that 26 percent of the farmers surveyed were reducing their use of pesticides thanks to genetically modified corn. Half the farmers planting the corn used no insecticides at all. "It would be a crime if those advantages [such as using fewer synthetic chemicals] were lost to a cynical campaign by those who use fear when science isn't on their side,"[70] Hurst says.

At the same time, there are also some public health concerns. One is allergies. For example, some people are allergic to peanuts. If a trait from a peanut, for example, is inserted into a vegetable crop, could the vegetable cause allergies as well? One study of a modified soybean seed showed that it had acquired an allergy-causing trait from a Brazil nut. However, Goklany points out that it is possible to test for such traits, as was done with the soybean. If such a trait is found, commercial production can be curtailed. And Adler observes that conventional plant breeding can also transfer allergies.

Another contention is that genetically modified crops will *not* reduce pesticide use. For instance, Novartis Seeds, one of the leading companies selling corn seeds with the Bt toxin, found that the bacterium worked in preventing the European corn borer from settling into the crops. However, sap-sucking insects attacked the plants instead. "Bt toxin has a rather narrow spectrum of activity, so you don't get control of all pests," says Walter Smolders, head of patents at Novartis Seeds.[71]

So, although the potential of genetically modified foods is great, traditional pesticides will not be replaced for a while. Until the concerns and questions are satisfactorily worked out, chemical pesticides and other farming techniques will be used.

## Conclusion

Change is a fact of life, no less in the case of pesticides as anywhere else. It appears that although pesticide use will continue for the foreseeable future, there will be declines in the amounts used. Responding to strict regulation, farmers and pesticide producers will deliberately use techniques that cut back on such chemicals. In addition, technologies are evolving that appear to require fewer pesticides.

Exactly what form agriculture will take cannot be predicted. However, strong regulation, continuing pressure from activist groups, and the need to keep crop yields high will lead to a mix of strategies that should enable farmers to feed a growing world population and reduce insect-borne diseases such as malaria without causing additional environmental harm.

 Notes

## Chapter 1: Why the Controversy over Pesticide Use?

1. Thomas Dunlap, *DDT: Scientists, Citizens, and Public Policy.* Princeton, NJ: Princeton University Press, 1981, p. 37.

2. Christopher J. Bosso, *Pesticides and Politics: The Life Cycle of a Public Issue.* Pittsburgh, PA: University of Pittsburgh Press, 1987, p. 29.

3. Dunlap, *DDT,* p. 64.

4. Rachel Carson, *Silent Spring.* Boston: Houghton Mifflin, 1962. Reprinted, 1987, p. 2.

5. Carson, *Silent Spring,* p. 172.

6. William Hazeltine, Testimony, Committee on Agriculture, House of Representatives, Hearings, 92nd Cong., 1st sess. Washington, DC: U.S. Government Printing Office, 1971.

7. Jack Lewis, "The Birth of EPA," *EPA Journal,* November 1985. www.epa.gov.

8. E.M. Sweeney, "EPA Hearing Examiner's Recommendations and Findings Concerning DDT Hearings," April 25, 1972.

9. R. Cremlyn, *Pesticides: Preparation and Mode of Action.* Chichester, UK: John Wiley & Sons, 1978, p. 215.

10. National Research Council, *The Future Role of Pesticides in U.S. Agriculture.* Washington, DC: National Academy Press, 2000, p. 80.

11. Harland Austin, Julian E. Keil, and Philip Cole, "A Prospective Follow-Up Study of Cancer Mortality in Relation to Serum DDT," *American Journal of Public Health,* January 1989, p. 43.

12. Dunlap, *DDT,* p. 231.

13. Roger E. Meiners and Andrew P. Morriss, "DDT: An Issue of Property Rights," *PERC Reports.* Bozeman, MT: PERC, September 2001, p. 4.

14. Elizabeth Whelan, *Toxic Terror.* Buffalo, NY: Prometheus Books, 1993, p. 117.

# Chapter 2: Pesticides and Human Health

15. Clark W. Heath Jr., "Pesticides and Cancer Risk," *Cancer*, November 15, 1997, p. 1,887.

16. Gina Solomon, "Pesticides and Human Health: A Resource for Health Care Professionals," Santa Monica, CA: Physicians for Social Responsibility, 2000. www.psrla.org.

17. Quoted in Virginia Postrel, "Of Mice and Men," *Reason*, December 1991, p. 18.

18. Quoted in Donna U. Vogt, "The Delaney Dilemma: Regulating Pesticide Residues in Foods—Seminar Proceedings, March 16, 1993," Congressional Research Service Report for Congress (Summary). www.cnie.org.

19. Quoted in Karen Bowerman, "Tests Spark Pesticide Concern," *BBC News Online*, September 20, 2000. http://news.bbc.co.uk.

20. National Cancer Institute of Canada, Ad Hoc Panel on Pesticides and Cancer, "Report of a Panel on the Relationship Between Public Exposure to Pesticides and Cancer," *Cancer*, November 15, 1997, p. 2,019.

21. Michael Fumento, *Science Under Siege*. New York: William Morrow, 1993, p. 83.

22. Bjørn Lomborg, *The Skeptical Environmentalist*. Cambridge, UK: Cambridge University Press, 2001, p. 231.

23. Fumento, *Science Under Siege*, p. 78.

24. Bruce N. Ames and Lois Swirsky Gold, "The Causes and Prevention of Cancer: The Role of Environment," in Ronald Bailey, ed., *The True State of the Planet*. New York: The Free Press, 1995, p. 158.

25. Dennis Avery, *Saving the Planet with Pesticides and Plastic*. Indianapolis, IN: Hudson Institute, 1995, p. 131.

26. National Research Council, *Pesticides in the Diets of Infants and Children*. Washington, DC: National Academy Press, 1993, p. 1.

27. Kenneth Chilton and Stephen Huebner, "Questioning the Emphasis on Environmental Contaminants as a Significant Threat

to Children's Health." St. Louis: Center for the Study of American Business, December 1998, p. 5.

28. National Research Council, *Carcinogens and Anticarcinogens in the Human Diet*. Washington, DC: National Academy Press, 1996, p. 16.

29. Quoted in Reuters News Service, "Pesticides Linked to Male Infertility," July 26, 2001. www.msnbc.com.

30. Quoted in Janet Raloff, "Hormone Mimics: New Assessments Air," *Science News*, August 14, 1999, p. 101.

## Chapter 3: Pesticides and Agriculture

31. Bosso, *Pesticides and Politics*, p. 28.

32. Indur M. Goklany, "Economic Growth and the State of Humanity," *PERC Policy Series* PS-21. Bozeman, MT: PERC, April 2001, p. 4.

33. Blake Hurst, "Agriculture," *Encyclopedia of Business and Industry*, Richard D. Western, ed. Tarrytown, NY: Marshall Cavendish, forthcoming.

34. National Research Council, *Pesticides in the Diets of Infants and Children*, p. 1.

35. Indur M. Goklany, "The Pros and Cons of Modern Farming," *PERC Reports*. Bozeman, MT: PERC, March 2001, p. 12.

36. Joseph Collins, Frances Moore, and Peter Rosset, "Lessons from the Green Revolution: Do We Need New Technology to End Hunger?" *Tikkun*, March/April 2000. www.twnside.org.

37. Barbara Dinham, "Getting Off the Pesticide Treadmill," *Our Planet*, November 1996. www.ourplanet.com.

38. Food and Agriculture Organization, "Rome Declaration on World Food Security," November 1996. www.fao.org.

39. Hervé la Prairie, Speech at the International Conference on Organic Agriculture, Copenhagen, May 2, 1996.

40. Dennis Avery, *Saving the Planet with Pesticides and Plastic*, p. 167.

41. Robert Quinn, "Why I Am an Organic Farmer," *PERC Reports*. Bozeman, MT: PERC, March 1999, p. 7.

## Chapter 4: Pesticides and Disease

42. Janet Raloff, "The Case for DDT," *Science News Online,* July 1, 2001. www.sciencenews.org.

43. Ellen Ruppel Shell, "Resurgence of a Deadly Disease," *Atlantic Monthly,* August 1997, p. 49.

44. Dyann F. Wirth and Jacqueline Cattani, "Winning the War Against Malaria," *Technology Review,* August/September, 1997, p. 54.

45. Shell, "Resurgence of a Deadly Disease," p. 48.

46. Quoted in Shell, "Resurgence of a Deadly Disease," p. 48.

47. Quoted in Environmental News Network, "Group Calls for Worldwide DDT Ban," January 29, 1999. http://cgi.cnn.com.

48. Quoted in Environmental News Network, January 29, 1999.

49. Harold M. Koenig, Foreword to Richard Tren and Roger Bate, *Malaria and the DDT Story.* London: The Institute of Economic Affairs, 2001, p. 11.

50. Quoted in Rageh Omaar, "Environmentalists Threaten Malaria Fight," *BBC News,* August 30, 2000. http://news.bbc.co.uk.

51. United Nations International Children's Emergency Fund (UNICEF), *Rolling Back Malaria.* New York: UNICEF, 1999, p. 8.

52. Roger E. Meiners and Andrew P. Morriss, "Pesticides and Property Rights," *PERC Policy Series.* Bozeman, MT: PERC, May 2001, p. 17.

53. IAPAC website. www.iapac.org.

54. Quoted in IAPAC website.

55. Richard Tren and Roger Bate, *Malaria and the DDT Story.* London: The Institute of Economic Affairs, 2001, p. 11.

56. Jane E. Brody, "More than Just a Nuisance, a Virtuoso of Disease," *New York Times,* August 7, 2001, p. F1.

## Chapter 5: The Future of Pesticides

57. Ashwin C. Shroff, "Strategy for Developing the Pesticides Industry," *Financial Express* (Bombay), July 8, 1999. www.express india.com.

58. Quoted in Fred Alvarez, "Jury Still Out on Pesticide Substitute Trials," *Los Angeles Times,* October 25, 1999. www.latimes.com.

59. Michael Fumento, "EPA Must Decide Whether Food Quality Act Protects Kids or Bugs," April 28, 1998. www.fumento.com.

60. Quoted in *Chemical Week,* "Is EPA Stifling Development of New Pesticides?" October 29, 1975, p. 25.

61. Mary Louise Flint and Robert van den Bosch, *Introduction to Integrated Pest Management.* New York: Plenum Press, 1981, p. 6.

62. Flint and van den Bosch, *Introduction to Integrated Pest Management,* p. 7.

63. Quoted in Anonymous, "IPM Basics: Monitoring and IPM," *IPM Almanac.* www.ipmalmanac.com.

64. Avery, *Saving the World with Pesticides and Plastic,* p. 13.

65. Gordon Conway and Gary Toenniessen, "Feeding the World in the 21st Century," *Nature,* December 2, 1999. www.biotech -info.net.

66. Indur M. Goklany, *The Precautionary Principle,* Washington, DC: Cato Institute, 2001, p. 40.

67. Goklany, "Applying the Precautionary Principle to Genetically Modified Crops," p. 18.

68. Jonathan Adler, "More Sorry than Safe: Assessing the Precautionary Principle and the Proposed International Biosafety Protocol," *Texas International Law Journal,* Spring 2000, p. 179.

69. Blake Hurst, "No Bio-Corn on My Farm This Year," *PERC Reports.* Bozeman, MT: PERC, March 2000, p. 6.

70. Hurst, "No Bio-Corn on My Farm This Year," p. 7.

71. Quoted in Andy Coghlan and Barry Fox, "Keep That Spray: Crops Made Resistant to Pests Still Do Better with Chemicals," *New Scientist,* December 18, 1999, p. 5.

# Glossary

**Agricultural technology:** modern devices used in agriculture such as tractors, hybrid seeds, fertilizers, and pesticides.

**Biological control:** controlling pests with the use of one or more living things; for example, some farmers use spiders in their crops because they eat insects.

**Biopesticides:** pesticides found in nature, such as bacteria or chemicals produced naturally by plants; if these pesticides are synthesized, they are copies of a natural substance.

**Bt:** *Bacillus thuringiensis,* a bacterium (microscopic organism) that kills insects; used in agriculture to control pests biologically.

**Cancer:** a disease that occurs when cell growth is uncontrolled.

**Carcinogen:** chemical, physical, or biological agent that can cause cancer.

**Chloroquine:** a medicine used to prevent and treat malaria.

**Cultivation control:** limiting pests through physical action such as picking insects off plants by hand.

**Epidemiology:** a scientific discipline that attempts to identify the causes of disease in a population.

**Fungicides:** chemicals used to kill fungi.

**Fungus (pl., fungi):** a plantlike organism that lives by absorbing nutrients from organic matter rather than through photosynthesis.

**Genetic engineering (or genetic modification):** altering an organism's hereditary characteristics, usually to produce more desirable traits, typically by inserting desirable genes directly into the organism.

**Green Revolution:** the introduction of modern farming techniques and seeds during the second half of the twentieth century that produced higher yielding, more pest-resistant varieties of crops.

**Herbicides:** chemicals used to kill plants, usually weeds.

**Hybrid:** a plant produced from a cross between two plants with different genetic traits.

**Insecticides:** chemicals used to kill insects.

**Integrated Pest Management (IPM):** a method of controlling pests that combines a variety of techniques including biological and physical control; pesticides may be used but not as the primary tool.

**Malaria:** an infection of the red blood cells transmitted by the bite of a mosquito.

**Monoculture:** production of the same crops on great expanses of land, year after year.

**Mycotoxin:** a toxic substance produced by a fungus.

**Nematode:** parasitic worm that may live in plants, animals, soil, or water.

**Organic:** grown without the use of synthetic (man-made) chemicals.

**Organochlorine:** pesticide containing the element chlorine; DDT is an example.

**Organophosphates:** pesticides containing phosphorus; parathion is an example.

**Parkinson's disease:** a brain disorder characterized by trembling, stiffness, slowness of movement, and impaired balance and coordination.

**Pesticide treadmill:** the process of using more and more pesticides because pests become resistant to a pesticide.

**Pheromones:** chemicals produced naturally by pests that attract other members of the species; the substances can be synthesized.

**Photosynthesis:** the process by which plants take in sunlight and create carbohydrates.

**Residues:** trace amounts of pesticides or other chemicals found on food.

**Toxic:** poisonous.

**Tumors:** a new and abnormal growth of cells.

**Typhus:** an infectious disease transmitted by a louse or a flea.

**West Nile virus:** an ultramicroscopic infectious agent transmitted by mosquitoes.

 For Further Reading

## Books

Rachel Carson, *Silent Spring*, 1962. Reprinted Boston: Houghton Mifflin, 1987. A classic in environmental literature. Carson gives account after account of possible outcomes of pesticide use in the United States, with specific attention paid to DDT.

Michael Fumento, *Science Under Siege*. New York: William Morrow, 1993. This book explores a variety of environmental worries, many of which have been exaggerated by the media and environmental activist campaigns.

Cathy Trost, *Elements of Risk: The Chemical Industry and Its Threat to America*. New York: Times Books, 1984. An exploration of the chemical industry in the United States that raises alarm about the dangers it poses.

Elizabeth Whelan, *Toxic Terror*. Buffalo, NY: Prometheus Books, 1993. Citing history and science, Whelan argues that Americans have been misled about the dangers of pesticides and other chemicals.

## Periodicals

Dennis Avery, "Why Greens Should Love Pesticides," *Wall Street Journal*, August 12, 1999.

Janet Raloff, "The Case for DDT: What Do You Do When a Dreaded Environmental Pollutant Saves Lives?" *Science News*, July 1, 2000.

## Internet Sources

Environmental Protection Agency, Office of Pesticide Programs. www.epa.gov.

Michael Fumento Reports. www.fumento.com.

The Pesticide Action Network. www.pan-uk.org.

The United Nations Food and Agriculture Organization. www.fao.org.

# Works Consulted

## Books

Bruce N. Ames and Lois Swirsky Gold, "The Causes and Prevention of Cancer: The Role of Environment." In Ronald Bailey, ed., *The True State of the Planet*. New York: Free Press, 1995.

Dennis Avery, *Saving the Planet with Pesticides and Plastic*. Indianapolis, IN: Hudson Institute, 1995.

Christopher J. Bosso, *Pesticides and Politics: The Life Cycle of a Public Issue*. Pittsburgh, PA: University of Pittsburgh Press, 1987.

Theo Colborn, Diane Dumanoski, John Peterson Myers, *Our Stolen Future*. New York: Plume, 1997.

Richard H. Craven, *Pests and Diseases*. Alexandria, VA: Time-Life Books, 1977.

R. Cremlyn, *Pesticides: Preparation and Mode of Action*. Chichester, UK: John Wiley and Sons, 1978.

Richard Doll and Richard Peto, *The Causes of Cancer*. Oxford, UK: Oxford University Press, 1986.

Mary Louise Flint and Robert van den Bosch, *Introduction to Integrated Pest Management*. New York: Plenum Press, 1981.

Indur M. Goklany, *The Precautionary Principle*. Washington, DC: Cato Institute, 2001.

Frank Graham Jr., *Since Silent Spring*. Boston: Houghton Mifflin, 1970.

Blake Hurst, "Agriculture," *Encyclopedia of Business and Industry*, Richard D. Western, ed. Tarrytown, NY: Marshall Cavendish, forthcoming.

Bjørn Lomborg, *The Skeptical Environmentalist*. Cambridge, UK: Cambridge University Press, 2001.

F.L. McEwen and G.R. Stephenson, *The Use and Significance of Pesticides in the Environment*. New York: John Wiley & Sons, 1979.

Anthony D. Miller, "Do Pesticide Scares Raise Cancer Rates?" *Global Food Progress*. Ed. Dennis T. Avery. Indianapolis: Hudson Institute, 1991.

National Research Council, *Carcinogens and Anticarcinogens in the Human Diet.* Washington, DC: National Academy Press, 1996.

National Research Council, *The Future Role of Pesticides in U.S. Agriculture.* Washington, DC: National Academy Press, 2000.

National Research Council, *Pesticides in the Diets of Infants and Children.* Washington, DC: National Academy Press, 1993.

E.C. Oerke, H.W. Dehne, F. Schönbeck, and A. Weber, *Crop Production and Crop Protection: Estimated Losses in Major Food and Cash Crops.* Amsterdam: Elsevier Science, 1999.

Richard Tren and Roger Bate, *Malaria and the DDT Story.* London: The Institute of Economic Affairs, 2001.

## Periodicals and Short Papers

Jonathan Adler, "More Sorry than Safe: Assessing the Precautionary Principle and the Proposed International Biosafety Protocol," *Texas International Law Journal,* Spring 2000.

Jonathan H. Adler, "Hidden Risks of Pesticide Bans," *Journal of Commerce,* September 1992.

Fred Alvarez, "Jury Still Out on Pesticide Substitute Trials," *Los Angeles Times,* October 25, 1999.

American Council on Science and Health, "From Mice to Men: The Benefits and Limitations of Animal Testing in Predicting Human Cancer Risk." New York, 1991.

American Institute for Cancer Research, "Food, Nutrition and the Prevention of Cancer: A Global Perspective." Washington, DC, 1997.

Per Pinstrup Andersen, "Modern Biotechnology and Small Farmers in Developing Countries," *IFPRI Research Perspectives.* Washington, DC: International Food Policy Research Institute, Fall 1999.

Amir Attaran and Rajendra Maharaj, "DDT for Malaria Control Should Not Be Banned," *British Medical Journal,* December 2, 2000.

*Audubon,* "The 42nd Annual Christmas Bird Census," January/ February 1942.

*Audubon,* "The 61st Annual Christmas Bird Census," January/ February 1961.

Harland Austin, Julian E. Keil, and Philip Cole, "A Prospective Follow-Up Study of Cancer Mortality in Relation to Serum DDT," *American Journal of Public Health,* January 1989.

Jane E. Brody, "More than Just a Nuisance, a Virtuoso of Disease," *New York Times,* August 7, 2001.

Fred Charatan, "Eight Die in Outbreak of Virus Spread from Birds," *British Medical Journal,* October 9, 1999.

*Chemical Week,* "Is EPA Stifling Development of New Pesticides?" October 29, 1975.

Kenneth Chilton and Stephen Huebner, "Questioning the Emphasis on Environmental Contaminants as a Significant Threat to Children's Health." St. Louis: Center for the Study of American Business, December 1998.

Andrew E. Czeizel et al., "Environmental Trichloron and Cluster of Congenital Abnormalities," *Lancet,* February 27, 1993.

General Accounting Office, "Pesticides: Adulterated Imported Foods Are Reaching U.S. Grocery Shelves." Washington, DC: U.S. Government Printing Office, 1992.

E.J. Gerberg and H. Wilcox III, "Environmental Assessment of Malaria and Control Projects Sri Lanka," Washington, DC: Agency for International Development, 1977.

Indur M. Goklany, "Economic Growth and the State of Humanity," *PERC Policy Series* PS-21. Bozeman, MT: PERC, April 2001.

Indur M. Goklany, "The Pros and Cons of Modern Farming," *PERC Reports.* Bozeman, MT: PERC, March 2001.

J.P. Grieco, N. Achee, R. Andre, and D. Roberts, "A Comparison of House Entering and Exiting Behavior of *Anopheles vestitipennis* Using Experimental Huts Sprayed with DDT or Deltamethrin in the Southern District of Toledo, Belize," *Journal of Vector Ecology,* June 2000.

Clark W. Heath Jr., "Pesticides and Cancer Risk," *Cancer,* November 15, 1997.

Tosihiko Hukuhara, Takahiko Hayakawa, and Arman Wijonarko, "Increased Baculovirus Susceptibility of Armyworm Larvae Feeding on Transgenic Rice Plants Expressing an Entomopoxvirus Gene," *Nature Biotechnology*, November 1999.

Blake Hurst, "No Bio-Corn on My Farm This Year," *PERC Reports*. Bozeman, MT: PERC, March 2000.

Ron Knutson, Ed Smith, and Robert Taylor, "Pesticide Elimination Would Lead to More Imported Food." College Station Texas A&M University's Agricultural and Food Policy Center, May 1999.

B. Lee and P. Groth, "Scabies: Transcutaneous Poisoning During Treatment," *Pediatrics*, April 1977.

Jonathan Norton Leonard, "Rachel Carson Dies of Cancer," *New York Times*, April 15, 1964.

Ben Lieberman, "Why Methyl Bromide Is Crucial," *Journal of Commerce*, January 3, 1996.

Michael Lipton, "Reviving Global Poverty Reduction: What Role for Genetically Modified Plants?" Working paper No. 6. Brighton, UK: Poverty Research Unit at Sussex (PRUS), April 2000.

Richard Liroff, "Reduction and Elimination of DDT Should Proceed Slowly," *British Medical Journal*, December 2, 2000.

Leslie London and Andrea Rother, "People, Pesticides and the Environment: Who Bears the Brunt of Backward Policy in South Africa?" *New Solutions: A Journal of Environmental and Occupational Health Policy*, No. 4, 2000.

Roger E. Meiners and Andrew P. Morriss, "DDT: An Issue of Property Rights," *PERC Reports*. Bozeman, MT: PERC, September 2001.

Roger E. Meiners and Andrew P. Morriss, "Pesticides and Property Rights," *PERC Policy Series*. Bozeman, MT: PERC, May 2001.

National Cancer Institute of Canada, Ad Hoc Panel on Pesticides and Cancer, "Report of a Panel on the Relationship Between Public Exposure to Pesticides and Cancer," *Cancer*, November 15, 1997.

Natural Resources Defense Council, "Intolerable Risk: Pesticides in Our Children's Food." Washington, DC, 1989.

Penny Olsen, Phil Fuller, and T.G. Marples, "Pesticide-Related Eggshell Thinning in Australian Raptors," *EMU* (Journal of the Royal Australasian Ornithologists Union), March 1993.

David Pimentel et al., "Environmental and Economic Costs of Pesticide Use," *BioScience,* October 1992.

Virginia Postrel, "Of Mice and Men," *Reason,* December 1991.

Robert Quinn, "Why I Am an Organic Farmer," *PERC Reports.* Bozeman, MT: PERC, March 1999.

Janet Raloff, "Hormone Mimics: New Assessments Air," *Science News,* August 14, 1999.

D. R. Roberts, S. Manguin, and J. Mouchet, "DDT House Spraying and Re-Emerging Malaria," *Lancet,* July 22, 2000.

Linda-Jo Schierow, "Pesticide Residue Regulation: Analysis of Food Quality Protection Act Implementation." Washington, DC: Congressional Research Service Report RS20043, August 3, 1999.

Barry Schlachter, "Malaria on Rise in Many Third World Areas," Associated Press, May 6, 1985.

Ellen Ruppel Shell, "Resurgence of a Deadly Disease," *Atlantic Monthly,* August 1997.

Pat Sidley, "Malaria Epidemic Expected in Mozambique," *British Medical Journal,* March 11, 2000.

M. Thiruchelvam et al., "The Nigrostriatal Dopaminergic System as a Preferential Target of Repeated Exposures to Combined Paraquat and Maneb: Implications for Parkinson's Disease," *Journal of Neuroscience,* December 15, 2000.

Dyann F. Wirth and Jacqueline Cattani, "Winning the War Against Malaria," *Technology Review,* August/September 1997.

R. J. Zwiener and C.M. Ginsburg, "Organophosphate and Carbamate Poisoning in Infants and Children," *Pediatrics,* January 1988.

**Internet Sources**

Anonymous, "IPM Basics: Monitoring and IPM," *IPM Almanac.* www.ipmalmanac.com.

Anonymous, "Puffers Mean Pears Are Practically Pesticide-Free," *Gempler's IPM Solutions,* June 2001. www.ipmalmanac.com.

Karen Bowerman, "Tests Spark Pesticide Concern," *BBC News Online,* September 20, 2000. http://news.bbc.co.uk.

Centers for Disease Control and Prevention, "Seizures Temporally Associated with the Use of DEET Insect Repellant in New York and Connecticut," *Morbidity and Mortality Weekly Report,* October 6, 1989. www.cdc.gov.

Centers for Disease Control and Prevention, "West Nile Virus." www.cdc.gov.

Joseph Collins, Frances Moore, and Peter Rosset, "Lessons from the Green Revolution: Do We Need New Technology to End Hunger?" *Tikkun,* March/April 2000. www.twnside.org.

Gordon Conway and Gary Toenniessen, "Feeding the World in the 21st Century," *Nature,* December 2, 1999. www.biotech-info. net/conway2.html.

Barbara Dinham, "Getting Off the Pesticide Treadmill," *Our Planet,* November 1996. www.ourplanet.com.

Environmental News Network, "Group Calls for Worldwide DDT Ban," January 29, 1999. http://cgi.cnn.com.

Environmental Protection Agency, Office of Pesticide Programs, "Potential of Chemicals to Affect the Endocrine System," January 1997. www.epa.gov.

Environmental Protection Agency, Office of Pesticide Programs, "Prevention, Pesticides and Toxic Substances," 1998. www. epa.gov.

Environmental Protection Agency, Office of Pesticide Programs, "What 'Organically Grown' Means." www.epa.gov.

G.A. Fermin-Munoz et al., "Biotechnology: A New Era for Plant Pathology and Plant Protection," *APSnet,* May 2000. www.apsnet.org.

Food and Agriculture Organization, "Rome Declaration on World Food Security," November 1996. www.fao.org.

Michael Fumento, "EPA Must Decide Whether Food Quality Act Protects Kids or Bugs," April 28, 1998. www.fumento.com.

Deepak Gajurel, "Obsolete Hazardous Pesticides Poison Nepal," Environment News Service, April 2000. http://ens.lycos.com.

Edward Groth III, Charles M. Benbrook, and Karen Lutz, "Update: Pesticides in Children's Foods," Washington, DC: Consumers Union, May 2000. www.ecologic-ipm.com.

IAPAC website. www.iapac.org.

Institute for Food and Development Policy, "Twelve Myths About Hunger," *Backgrounder,* Summer 1998. www.foodfirst.org.

Jack Lewis, "The Birth of EPA," *EPA Journal,* November 1985. www.epa.gov.

Claude Morgan, "Debating DDT," Environmental News Network, November 11, 1999. www.enn.com.

National Center for Public Policy Research, "Organic Labeling Study," May 2000. www.nationalcenter.org.

Gaylord Nelson, "The History of Earth Day," The Wilderness Society, 2001. www.earthday.wilderness.org.

Rageh Omaar, "Environmentalists Threaten Malaria Fight," *BBC News,* August 30, 2000. http://news.bbc.co.uk.

Janet Raloff, "The Case for DDT," *Science News Online,* July 1, 2001. www.sciencenews.org.

Reuters News Service, "Pesticides Linked to Male Infertility," July 26, 2001. www.msnbc.com.

Ashwin C. Shroff, "Strategy for Developing the Pesticides Industry," *Financial Express* (Bombay), July 8, 1999. www.expressindia.com.

Gina Solomon, "Pesticides and Human Health: A Resource for Health Care Professionals," Santa Monica, CA: Physicians for Social Responsibility, 2000. www.psrla.org.

Donna U. Vogt, "The Delaney Dilemma: Regulating Pesticide Residues in Foods—Seminar Proceedings, March 16, 1993," Congressional Research Service Report for Congress (Summary). www.cnie.org.

World Health Organization, "Malaria," Fact Sheet No. 94, October 1998. www.who.int/inf-fs/en/fact094.html.

## Other

Committee on Agriculture, House of Representatives, Hearings, 92nd Cong., 1st session: Washington, DC: U.S. Government Printing Office, 1971.

Government of the Philippines, "Philippine Case Study: A Developing Country's Perspective on POPs." Intergovernmental Forum on Chemical Safety Meeting on POPs, Manila, Philippines, June 17–19, 1996.

Hervé la Prairie, Speech at the International Conference on Organic Agriculture, Copenhagen, May 2, 1996.

E.M. Sweeney, "EPA Hearing Examiner's Recommendations and Findings Concerning DDT Hearings," April 25, 1972.

United Nations International Children's Emergency Fund (UNICEF), *Rolling Back Malaria*. New York: UNICEF, 1999.

U.S. Food and Drug Administration, Center for Food Safety and Applied Nutrition Pesticide Program, "Residue Monitoring 1999," April 2000.

World Health Organization, "Viral Meningitis in Romania— Update 3," September 24, 1996.

World Wildlife Fund, "Reducing Reliance on Pesticides in Great Lakes Basin Agriculture." Washington, DC, 1997.

# Acknowledgments

Critical Thinking About Environmental Issues: *Pesticides,* by Samantha Beres, belongs to a new series of books designed to help students address environmental issues, which all too often are treated with emotion rather than objectivity. The editor of the series, Jane S. Shaw, appreciates the support of two key people: Terry L. Anderson, executive director of PERC—the Center for Free Market Environmentalism—in Bozeman, Montana, and Fred L. Smith Jr., president of the Competitive Enterprise Institute in Washington, DC. They recognize the value of treating these issues in a careful, balanced way and allowed the author and editor to explore the best way to bring fairness and accuracy to these topics. Shaw also thanks Michael Sanera for his role in initiating the series. Samantha Beres appreciates the comments of Carl Winter, director of the FoodSafe Program of the Department of Food Science and Technology, University of California at Davis.

# Index

# Picture Credits

Cover Photo: © John Foxx; cover inset photo credits (from top): © John Foxx; © Flat Earth; © John Foxx; © John Foxx; © Flat Earth; © John Foxx

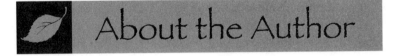

# About the Author

Samantha Beres is a freelance writer living in Chimayo, New Mexico. For seven years she has worked for the American Association for the Advancement of Science (AAAS), first as an associate editor and currently as a creator of online science lessons. She has produced educational videos and hands-on science materials for the Challenger Center for Space Science Education. She has written seven science books for children. Her articles have appeared in *Astronomy Magazine* and *Scientific American Explorations* and on Discovery Online. In her spare time she dances, writes poetry, runs, and reupholsters furniture.